THE CARING CHURCH

THE CARING CHURCH

OLIVER MCMAHAN

Pathway
PRESS

Scripture quotations are taken from the *New King James Version.* Copyright © 1979, 1980, 1982, 1990, 1995, Thomas Nelson Inc., Publishers.

Book Editor: Wanda Griffith
Editorial Assistant: Tammy Hatfield
Copy Editors: Cresta Shawver
Oreeda Burnette
Inside Layout: Mark Shuler

Library of Congress Catalog Card Number: 2002103551
ISBN: 0-87148-487-0
Copyright © 2002 by Pathway Press
Cleveland, Tennessee 37311
All Rights Reserved
Printed in the United States of America

DEDICATION

To my family, my first line of care as a believer and as a part of His church.

My wife,

Martha,

daughter,

Holly,

son and daughter-in-law,

Jonathan and Heather,

and three granddaughters,

Haley Marie, Sarah Beth and Olivia Rose

CONTENTS

Acknowledgments

I would like to thank Dr. John Nichols, international executive director of Care Ministries for the Church of God International, and John Gregory, chairman of the Board of Directors for King Pharmaceuticals, for their leadership and partnership in care and benevolence ministries in the church worldwide.

Thank you, Dr. Dan Boling, director of publications, Dr. Bill George, editor in chief, Marcus V. Hand, editor at large, and the entire Pathway team for your ministry of publishing.

Thank you, Dr. Donald M. Walker, president, and the community of the Church of God Theological Seminary colleagues and students, including Keena Warren, my assistant.

Thank you to Gary Sears, senior pastor, and the congregation of Mount Olive Ministries; and Shea Hughes, senior pastor and congregation of Mount Olive East Ministries for the opportunity to have ministered as senior associate pastor and supervisor with you.

FOREWORD

Warning! This book is not for the fainthearted. Dr. McMahan tells us that laboring as Christ labored requires us to roll up our sleeves and get our hands dirty. Kingdom work requires fortitude. Early on he asks, "Where do we find the Kingdom? On the showroom floor when God finally blesses us with a new car? In the boardroom at work when our project wins approval? Or is it in the sanctuary when we lose sight of those around us and we think only of Jesus? Sorry, but that is not necessarily the Kingdom. Instead, Kingdom work is carrying out the mandate of Matthew 25 and James 1:27."

Working in the Kingdom requires us to visit the sick, help the poor, and remember the prisoner, the widow and the orphan. This is doing the work of our Master, and this kind of work is not always popular. Our Lord was constantly helping those about Him and speaking to the needs of the poor. The author asks, "What if Mary and Joseph did not show up at the door of the church, but you just heard about a couple in the community looking for food, clothing and shelter? Would there be a team from your church to reach them?"

Helping people outside the church is the thesis of his book, and this is what we like about Dr. McMahan's writing. We believe, as he does, that Matthew 25 is a mandate to the local church. The congregation that fully represents Christ must reach outside its walls to the hurting, the sick, the incarcerated, the hungry and the destitute.

When the church puts forth a genuine effort to help sinners, we may be misunderstood by some people. Even our

Lord was rejected by popular opinion and despised because He reached out to the hurting. Still, He constantly restored the fallen and those who had failed. Christ did not come just to encourage the believer, although He does that regularly, but Jesus' main purpose was to seek, to save and to help the lost, the poor, the widows and the orphans.

We believe the church that genuinely cares will endeavor to help those in spiritual and physical need. The very nature of caring demands it. In the eyes of some, the caring church is a congregation at risk. But the Lord Jesus himself identified with the despised, the sinner, the rejected and the poor.

We heartily recommend this book to you. Oliver McMahan is a learned man who leans not just on his academic preparation, but also on his wide experience as a successful pastor. His teaching as a seminary professor coupled with his pastoral success has uniquely prepared him to author this significant work.

But he is more than an academician. He writes with a heart throbbing for his reader to be constantly aware of those in need. He preaches like he writes. His constant emphasis in the pulpit on caring has catapulted him to wide recognition as a preacher genuinely concerned for others. We have needed for someone with the stature of Dr. McMahan to pour out his heart on the theme of caring like Jesus cares. We believe this volume will burden your heart for the needy in your community.

Dr. John D. Nichols
International Executive Director
Care Ministries

John Gregory
Chairman, Board of Directors
King Pharmaceuticals, Inc.

1

THE SEARCH FOR A CARING CHURCH

Where is the God-focused church that not only believes but also cares? The local congregation has so many priorities, we are left to wonder if the people who believe really care. Picture this scenario.

Scene 1: You walk through the front doors of a church and meet a smiling greeter who says one, two, perhaps five words. "Hello! Welcome to our church!" An even bigger smile follows. The greeter shakes your hand, and puts a piece of paper in the other one. It is the bulletin for the morning service. Whether *you* say anything or not is beside the point. The greeter has done his or her job, which is to give you a greeting. The greeter's duty is not to listen or exchange communication, much less receive any personal information about you or your family. Scene 1 is completed because you have been greeted.

Scene 2: A door opens into a large room. All the people in this room sit facing the stage. People look at the band, the preacher and the choir, but never at each other. Interaction is not their purpose; they are there to watch the front of the auditorium and see what happens. Thus the action is completed in Scene 2.

Scene 3: Church is where we "find the Lord," right? Pay attention. Don't let any noisy children distract you. In fact, put them in their own service in another location—outside the sanctuary. Don't show any emotion in church; you have come to "learn about the Lord." You have had to face the perils of mean, cruel people in the world, but here you can get away from them in the "sanctuary" of the Lord.

You finally settle into a pew, fasten your hymnal and set the controls just where you want them. The general impression is that the church is not about people; people only keep us from serving the Lord.

Is this what we call *church*? Is this what we are looking for? Some three-step process that doesn't get in anyone's way? In reality, such ritual doesn't reach anyone. Church, as it is practiced today, is not supposed to be for *you*; rather, *you* are supposed to be for the church. "Give your praise." "Give your attention to the reading of the announcements." "Give in the offering." "Give yourselves to the reading of the Word." And finally, "Give of yourself this week."

Go home. Go to work. Do not pass "go." And be sure to come back to church next Sunday.

Why People Don't Care
Make no mistake, the church is running. Sadly,

people are, too. But why are they running away from the local church?

The problem is that no one really cares. Sunday school superintendents have become strategy technicians. Church goals are organizational position statements. Discernment translates into assessment. Budgets are resource profiles. What was once a handful of people on a street corner meeting for prayer has become a technical marvel penetrating the new century.

What do we really want from church? What are we looking for?

Obviously, in many congregations all the dials are set and the meters are being properly regulated, but no one is at the controls. We have attempted to prepare the church for the 21st century, but the body is losing its pulse. Organization thrives in today's parish office, but fellowship in the parish has become nonexistent. How can we take the time to answer people's questions when we are due at a meeting to decide whether or not we have a vision? The church must move on with all of its five-part organizational strategy in balance . . . while people wait in the hallways for our meetings to be adjourn.

I am describing a church that feels it is ready for the increasing significance of the 21st century, but has lost the soul of the first-century church. Is this what we are really looking for? The heart is the source of life; the flow from it sustains the rest of the body. So what is the heart of the church? What keeps the rest of the body functioning?

Some churches exist to preserve doctrine and evangelize the world, but this is not why people look for a church. Would your children attend your church if they had a choice? If you had a need of any kind, would you think of your church? You know where to go for food, for clothing, for medicine, but why do you go to church?

Expectations of Care

If you think I've missed the point, ask yourself how many people spoke to you the last time you visited a church . . . or even went to your home church. We may need to quit trying to defend church people. The tragic reality is that few people talk to anyone at church. When they do, it is usually to the same few, leaving most people saying mostly nothing to everyone they pass.

The bulletin prints the vision statement of the church, the mission of the church, the goals of the church, the strategy of the church, the budget of the church, the faith of the church, the activities of the church and the future of the church. It is all on paper, but where is it in reality?

To search for a caring church, I am not advocating that we sell all church buildings, put on sandals and don our robes. Sincerity is not a garment, and righteousness is more than an approach to life. What we see and do not see is the real problem of an uncaring church. Whether you call it vision or just plain insight, we look at our buildings, but do not really see the church. We see what we have come to expect the church to be. But our expectations have been shaped in a boardroom; our projections are based on surveys.

What good is it to see the world in need of Christ if we continue to pass by the lame who sit at our gated churches? Remember, the man who walked by Lazarus each day and called Abraham his spiritual father (Luke 16:19-31)? The people who passed by the man at the gate called Beautiful were on their way to worship (Acts 3).

In John 4, the disciples had gone to buy lunch in the small town of Sychar. In actuality, Christ had sent them to reap the harvest of ministry in that town (v. 38). There was so much need there that Jesus had to stay two full days to minister. The disciples walked by the woman at the well on the way to fill their stomachs. They passed by the needy, satisfied their hunger and later rebuffed Jesus because He was not ready to eat (vv. 31-33). It took a transformed, broken woman with an immoral reputation to show that there were people in town who needed care. She also demonstrated that there was something she could do about her need.

When the disciples finally burst out of the Upper Room, they were forever changed by the Holy Spirit. They began to see what the religion of Judaism could no longer see. Peter could see what the priests refused to see—that to the priests, religion meant, "Don't touch the lame." The crowds thought the lame were on the fringe of the culture of religion.

The power of Pentecost did not send the Upper Room congregation around the world first. The Spirit sent them first to the blind, the lame, the widows and the untouchables. When was the last time you saw the penniless listed among the givers in your church? Could a pauper be an elder in your church? Could a pauper even be accepted in your church? Could the untouchables be held in the arms of your congregation?

The Needy

Is there even room for the Savior in today's church, much less room for a family searching for a genuine community of care? The local church in the new millennium may be the "inn" from which the needy, including the Savior, are excluded. Often Jesus cited what the kingdom of God was to be. Where do we find the Kingdom? Is it on the showroom floor when God finally blesses us with a new car? Or is it in the boardroom at work when our project wins approval? Or is it in the sanctuary, where we lose sight of those around us and only think of Jesus?

Sorry! Jesus did not say you would find His Kingdom when you receive, accomplish or acquire. In fact, the Kingdom has little to do with you. The kingdom of Jesus is about others. But we rationalize: *OK. I've got it. The Kingdom is about others. I pray for so many people at church. I've told so many about Jesus. I always try to help others whenever and however I can.*

Jesus' reply was graphic. Matthew 25 says that when we go before Jesus after this life is over, He will make sure we understand His definition of the Kingdom. Not only will every knee bow and every tongue confess that Jesus Christ is Lord (see Philippians 2:10), but everyone will know what "pure religion" is (see James 1:27). It is not a role we play, or something we do on weekends. It is not even the doctrines we believe in.

Jesus will want to know, "Did you notice the lame, the imprisoned, the down-and-out, the rejected, the lonely or the hungry?" (see Matthew 25:31-46). He will want to know if we cared for the unusual, not for the familiar; for the failures, not the achievers; for those who stand out at church for all the wrong reasons. His concern will be for those on your list who are most likely to be forgotten. He will want to know if you helped people who kept on failing and couldn't seem to get it right. Some of them may even have ended up in jail, and they may be people you had rather forget.

We have long lists of things we want Jesus to remember about us on the final Judgment Day, but He will want to talk about the people we've met. Jesus' checklist will ask how many people we have ministered to who were hungry, thirsty, strangers, sick, in prison or without basic clothing.

How many in your church this Sunday will fall into one of these categories, and you will not even realize it? Do the people in your community who have these needs even think about coming to your church on Sunday? It may not be that the church is doing better, but that the people who are doing worse don't bother to come to church anymore. Why? Because when they do come they are a "problem" to us rather than the heart of "pure religion."

Still Searching

Still searching for a caring church? Most who do not attend church are probably on that same search. The problem may not be that church never enters their minds, but that church, the way it is today, frequently crosses their minds. They understand that they would be outsiders with little chance of breaking in. They know that Jesus would be in the building, but He would not be in the people who would never visit, clothe, stand by and care for the needy.

Actually, a caring church is a church at risk. Our cultures, both civil and religious, militate against a caring church. When you take in the poor, you might look second-rate. When you befriend the imprisoned, you may appear to be compromising. When you stand by sinners, you may be called sinful. The risk is to look less like an institution and more like Christ. Jesus was always at risk with the religious and civil crowd of His day. He was an advocate for the outcasts, He was present with those who were failures and He died with criminals.

What process transforms a church from complacency to care? The remaining chapters of this book outline a strategy for moving a congregation from the comfort of "church as usual" to the doorway of all ministry—care. Christ and the apostles stepped through this door when they reached out to the outcasts of religion. The disciples stepped through it when they left the Temple to find a lame man ignored at the Temple gate (Acts 3, 4). Christ stands at the same door today with the lonely, hurting and impoverished, waiting for the church to step forward and begin ministering with genuine care.

Conclusion

The searching church looks back as well as forward. Reconciliation keeps us caring about more than forward progress. The search for a caring church is risky, painful and may seem somewhat backward, but that may be where the care of the church is.

More than likely, however, the care of the church is the point at which you and a fellow believer reach out to each other in order to meet with God. The search for the caring church is very close to the question asked of Jesus, "Who is my neighbor?" (see Luke 10:25-37). The question for the church is, "Who is my church?"

The answer is also similar to the answer Jesus gave — the person by the side of the road of life that you would rather pass.

2

STARTING WITH THE HEART OF OUR FATHER

A church should be aware enough to know that care originated with the love of the heavenly Father. The Father gave His Son because He cared. The church must find its formative roots in the care of the Father. Genuine care is not a human service; it is a divine gift. Humans do not even know how to care for themselves. Care comes first from the action of God, not from the activity of individuals. Care from a pure motive comes only from God.

Care Starts Early

"Hi. We're the Smiths. I'm Bob and this is my wife, Terri. These are my children, Bobby Jr., Melody and Cassidy. Bobby is 2, Melody is a year old and Cassidy is 3 months."

The Smiths are a young family living in town, and Bob works hard to be a good father and provide for the family. Terri is working hard to take care of the family. She tried a part-time job; but with three small children, it was impossible to work outside the home.

They have been so busy with trips to the doctor and going to work that they have had little time to think about their faith. Lately, they've been thinking about getting back in church. Bob and Terri both grew up in church, but they drifted away during their teen years. Today, they barely make ends meet financially. Raising a young family with three children, they live in fear about what the future holds for them.

The Smiths finally mustered up the courage to make their way to the church on the corner this past weekend. They have visited other churches in recent years, but they drive by this church every day. Terri has felt for several months that they need to visit it. On this Sunday, the one day in the week they can sleep late, they get up early instead. It is especially difficult to get the kids up because all three of them were up late with colds. Bob and Terri have to scramble around the house to find something to wear. Since they haven't attended church much since they've been married, they just look for the best they can find. Terri is especially conscious about their clothes and appearance, wondering if the family will fit in with everyone else wearing their Sunday finest.

The Smiths did not come because someone invited them; they just felt the need to come. Fears about their family's future haunt them. With needs weighing heavily on their minds, they decided to do what they are not accustomed to doing. For some reason, they wonder whether the odds for a pleasant experience are against them.

Terri realizes that they are two months behind on their rent. Bob had been spending more time with his friends and less at home. She is afraid that they will have fewer and fewer chances to make it as a family if something doesn't happen to change their lives. She checked Friday, and there was only enough food to last until Tuesday. Bob does not get paid until Thursday. They have no money until then, and their credit is bad. She wonders if the landlord will kick them out on the street. They have no relatives in town; besides, it would probably create even more problems if they did.

The church on the corner is facing one of its biggest tests. The critical challenge is not whether to meet the budget or whether to cast a vision for another year's work. The test is whether the church will reach the Smiths. The arena is not the board-room, the choir loft or even the pulpit. The church will not be tested on how well it sings, preaches or prays. This test begins in the doorway of the church and continues in the busyness of the nursery and the chaos of the classroom.

The greeter sees the Smiths coming up the steps, struggling to carry the baby while holding on to the diaper bag and the little toddlers at the same time.

Meanwhile, the greeter has been looking for his boss all morning. He invited him to church and was excited when his supervisor told him he would try to come. What a wonderful thought—his boss might start coming to church! This man could really help the church, and it would be good for the church in the community.

"Hi, I'm Bob and this is my family," Bob says breathlessly while holding tightly to his son and daughter. Both children are awestruck at the big room in front of them, the noises and the people.

"Hi! Welcome," says the greeter, handing Bob a bulletin. Bob has no idea what the piece of paper is. His church didn't have bulletins when he was growing up. He has forgotten about nurseries as well. He only knows that his wife really wanted them to come to church. Terri is beginning to panic, because this is not the way she thought it would be. She had contemplated just sitting and listening to the preacher, and somehow things would get better for them.

Get the picture. They are about to be evicted from their apartment. They have no money, average clothes and two days of food left at home. The enormous pressures of perhaps not being able to make it as a family has hit them hard. They stand in the foyer of the church, wanting desperately to climb out of poverty and despair, thinking that the church can change their lives for the better.

The church has worked hard in meetings and strategy sessions to figure out how it can effectively reach the community with the gospel of Christ, but the leaders have prepared for a Sunday service with only singing and preaching. The people are all dressed up and ready to follow the order of service today, to really have church. The Smiths want a life change; the church wants to have a service.

How Is the Church to Know?

How close does your church come to caring for families in need today? If the Smiths came to you this Sunday searching for a caring church, would your church's activities match their search? The Smiths were thinking about an answer that morning that would change their circumstances. Could the greeter, the choir or the sermon change them? The church wants to change their souls and spirits, but the Smiths are looking for more. Would the church's caring for this family end with a song and a prayer? Would the church have another opportunity next Sunday, or would the Smiths be out of their apartment by then?

Much of the church's mission today is not rooted in care. While visitors come to church wanting to be cared for, council members develop budgets to care for the buildings, programs and maintenance. Churches need to keep the lights on and pay the bills, but so do visitors who muster enough courage to visit on a day they usually spend somewhere else. Should a program in the church start by asking what we need or by asking what do the Smiths of the world need?

Where Does Care Come From?

The origin of care in the church is rooted in the care of the Father. We were in need, in desperate need. The heavenly Father heard and saw that need. He shaped His response around our broken, desperate condition, applying His ministry where we hurt. We did not come to Him before He came to us. He took the first step, because He was aware of our sorrows and griefs. He was not wondering whether we would ever fit into His kingdom. Rather, He built His kingdom, making sure it would fit us.

The Father gave His Son to die on Calvary because of His love and care for us while we were in need. Christ cared for us before we knew how to care for Him. We care for Him, but it is only possible because He first cared for us. Care is a step taken first by God. Correspondingly, care for the hurting and needy does not fully occur unless a church extends the heavenly Father's care and takes the first step.

The preservation of the church is not an act of care, and neither is the maintenance of a program. Preservation and maintenance are important in maintaining an institution. Humanity doesn't know how to fully care for itself. We always start with self-preservation, or the enterprise of maintenance. *Taking care* of others does not equip us to *care for* others. Our resources for care are not stored up or cultivated. Rather, God and His care are our first resource. We are able to care because God cares for us.

Care is the emptying of oneself rather than the building up of oneself. The Father gave His Son, who left the splendor and security of heaven so that He might indwell and care for humans (see Philippians 2). The church certainly has a role to play in the care it gives, but that care must first be shaped by the care of the Father. We care for others with the same compassion that we have received from God (see 1 Corinthians 2:3-5). The Father's care shapes the church's heart after His own heart. It shapes the cup of water given to those in need into a God-sized portion. The Father's care sets the sights of the church so that it *looks* for, rather than waits for, the hurting.

Stop, Look and Reach Out

The church in Corinth had many problems; however, it was known for its care. You may wonder why such a troubled church is even mentioned in Scripture. Why would a church with relational problems, internal strife and trouble with the courts merit such a prominent place in the New Testament? Paul gives us some indication when he applauds the Corinthian church for its care. In 2 Corinthians 1:7-11 Paul notes this about the Corinthian church:

> Our hope for you is steadfast, because we know that as you are partakers of the sufferings, so also you will partake of the consolation. For we do not want you to be ignorant, brethren, of our trouble which came to us in Asia: that we were burdened beyond measure, above strength, so that we despaired even of life. Yes, we had the sentence of death in ourselves, that we should not trust in ourselves but in God who raises the dead, who delivered us from so great a death, and does deliver us; in whom we trust that He will still deliver us, you also helping together in prayer for us, that thanks may be given by many persons on our behalf for the gift granted to us through many.

Paul's steadfast hope was in a church that did not ignore his trouble. They knew the pains of strife and need. They were surrounded by the wealth of one of the richest trading cities of the Roman Empire, but they were also well aware of the poverty of many around them. They had the sensitivity to understand the anguish of Paul when his life was seriously threatened. What does it take for a church to notice the needs, the fears and even the threats being faced by those around it?

In Luke 16, a wealthy and religious man ignored opportunities to care every day. His clothes were the best in town. *Purple* in verse 19 was a term for a rare, highly traded fabric that came from the trading routes of the East. *Fine linen* (v. 19) referred to the silk-like fabric of his undergarments. The Scripture indicates his wealth by underscoring the fact that he "fared sumptuously" (v. 19). He was a business-deal maker. Daily, his stock was up and he received the best breaks in life. We know he was religious because in verses 24 and 25 he called Abraham "father" and Abraham addressed him as "son."

Every day this fortunate and seemingly devout man passed by Lazarus. Lazarus was like the Smiths, only worse. He lay by the gateway to the rich man's residence (v. 20). The implication is that the man of wealth passed through the gate every day. The implication is that Lazarus could not go anywhere, so he was probably lame in some way. Further, he had been *laid* there, a word indicating a harsh circumstance, similar to the modern phrase "to be left there."

Finally, Lazarus was in constant pain—covered from head to toe with open ulcerations that would not heal (v. 20). The reference to dogs licking his wounds is both terrible and sympathetic for while they were dogs, they provided an ironic comfort by licking his wounds (v. 21). What a pitiful state.

Lazarus was left with only a degenerating form of pity that demeaned him as a human being. He only had the hope that the crumbs from the rich man's table might come to him (v. 21). Everything about him pointed to pain and neglect—two strange bedfellows that encourage each other. Neglect feeds pain, and pain isolates one to a life of neglect.

Changed by What You See

Do the unchurched see the local church around the corner "faring sumptuously"—parading its order of service before the community week after week? More people look at the church than the average congregation realizes. They see a group of people who have a lot of material things. They see them clothed, happy and well-fed. While the church enjoys the blessings of God, the unchurched in need, who are desperate and hurting, see believers through the lens of pain, poverty and crisis. Somehow the gap must be bridged.

How can the church on the corner change from one that cares and has a few ministries, to one that is actually a caring church? How can it bridge the gap between the hurting and unchurched, and the blessed within the church? I repeat: A caring church is much more than a church with a care ministry. What will it take for persons in their greatest hour of need to turn to the church, instead of waiting and suffering until they have nowhere else to turn?

In this book, each chapter will propose specific suggestions for a local church to implement in order to experience a transformation of care. The suggestions are not just about including a line on a budget, adding another ministry, holding a conference, conducting a special service or having a guest speaker. All of these things are necessary, but they will not transform the church into a caring force in the community. A caring church is birthed when the inner workings, priorities and actions of the congregation as a whole change.

The church has eyes that direct the goings and comings of the body, just as sight directs an individual through the day. The perspective of the church is called its "vision." The vision clarifies how the church views itself and its purpose. Just as the spirit is the eye of the soul, the vision of a church is the eye of its heart. Just as the lens of the eyes tell what is around the individual, the vision of a church tells the church what the body will see, where its priorities are and the direction its future will take.

Tragically, this first important step in church transformation — getting in touch with your church's vision — focuses all too often on only the successes of the church. What will our attendance be? What will our income be? What will our buildings look like? Consequently, the church looks only at numbers, finances and facilities. The boards and elders who first peer into the dark glass of a church's vision argue that these are the basics. That is, you have to have people, finances and buildings to run a church.

An important administrative principle in a church is to recognize what is necessary, but also secondary. Some things may be absolutely vital to a church — the church cannot do without them — yet they are secondary. One such item is a place to meet. Another is finance. Still another is a plan, a direction. Remember, something secondary will always be secondary. If the secondary thing is made the primary mission of the church, regardless of its value, that same thing can become a threat to the church.

For example, financial stability, though a necessary component of a church, is still a secondary value of the church when compared to other values. As the main priority, finances can turn a church into a brokerage firm of spiritual commodities, rather than a devout place of service where the people of God fulfill their calling. A church may not go under because of financial irresponsibility, but it will cease to be a center of care and become ungodly if finances become the focus of the church.

What focus is central in the church? This issue is a vital question and presses the importance of care in the local body. The position of this book is that care is at the center of the church's mission. The road to transforming a local church into a caring church, not merely a church having a care ministry, is to make care central to the guiding vision of the church. The church strays from its center when the Smiths of the world are secondary to the church's concerns about its financial responsibilities. The church should do both—care for the Smiths and its own finances—but it must decide which comes first and which is more important. The concern that is more valuable and closer to its center will direct the church's vision of what God has for it to do in the world.

The Search Continues

Look again at the Smiths. How pleasing it would be to the heavenly Father if the greeter's first thoughts were, *Praise the Lord, this is just what we have been waiting for—a new family in need. Here is someone to whom we can minister.*

What would happen if the first words of the greeter would be, "We're so glad you chose to come to church today. Can I help you? I see you have an infant. Would you feel comfortable letting our nursery helpers assist you? You have children. They may enjoy our children's classes and children's church. May I escort you to the children's area and introduce you to the children's teachers?"

What would happen if the greeter were also an escort who would commit to the Smiths: "I would enjoy helping *you* be seated, I will sit with you if you'd like." What if someone in the church was able to actually perceive, or even converse with, the Smiths about their needs? Even more wonderful, what if the Smiths actually felt the freedom to share their need with someone that day?

This is a lot to accomplish in one service. But the odds are that this visit will be the only opportunity the church has with the Smiths. Statistics show that most visitors do not return; many have already had a negative experience before they visit a church. Reaching the world, the county or the community is impossible if a church cannot demonstrate that it cares within its four walls. Before visitors go to the altar, before they are touched by a sermon or moved by a song, they have probably already decided if they have finally found a caring church.

The search for a caring church begins with the vision of that church—what it sees, the guiding light at the center of its values. The process of transforming a congregation into a caring church begins by making care central in the church's vision. That vision can guide every person in the congregation onto the pathway of care. It will become a beacon going out into the community, lighting the path to real, genuine care.

STRATEGIC TRANSFORMATION STEP
Develop a vision statement that makes care the gateway for all ministry.

PROCEDURE TO DEVELOP
Utilize care to increase the church's ability to perceive Christ.

IMPLICATIONS FOR CARE
The scope of care is guided by the church's vision of Christ as He walked on Earth.

3

BROKEN TO BE POURED OUT

The New Testament church is a suffering church. Today's church, however, avoids brokenness while equating health with relief, strength with painlessness and reconciliation with burden and reproof. Instead of seeing the Cross as a broken vessel, they only view it as a quick and easy solution for today's situations. We often act as though we are merely opting for holiness in a "Cross-less" pursuit.

Pain is not the great escape of the church; rather, it is the gateway to care. Following Jesus is more than writing a mission statement; it is moving to travail for the world. The ministry of care can only be realized by passing through the doorway of brokenness. The church must embrace this concept, not escape it, for true compassion is only felt as we are broken.

Is a Ramp Enough?

We care, We love you and *We miss you* are phrases

commonly used in the church community. So are
have faith, draw close to God and *be open to the Spirit.*
Words that often describe the goals of our spirituality
are *stronger, bigger* and *better.* These words are also the
standard by which we frequently measure our
churches. What if we were told that *marred, weak* and
broken were the new words to be sought after in the
church? No one would want these words, for they
describe images we avoid. They tell us about places in
the heart we feel are best left alone.

Meet Mary. Her face is bruised, especially around
the eyes. She wears a long-sleeved blouse and
slacks to church. She doesn't seem to lift her left arm
much, and winces when she takes her seat. She
doesn't look up at you; instead she purposely looks
down and away. Others in the church notice her.
Still more walk right past her.

Mary's condition is serious. She fought with her
husband last night, and it was hardly a fair fight. He
is a stout, 200-pound man, and she weighs in at a
scant 120. As blows from her husband struck her, she
stood feeling guilty from the onslaught of his verbal
denigration as well as from the physical beating.
Some in church notice her, guessing what may have
happened. They wonder, *Why did she even come?
Doesn't she know how awful she looks? What did she do to
get herself in such a mess?*

Then Martha comes up the ramp at the side of the
church with her husband in a wheelchair. He is 72,
and she is 71. A stroke last year left him unable to
walk, the limbs on the left side of his body para-
lyzed. Martha is not very good with the wheelchair
yet. Her husband can get in and out of it, but she

finds it difficult to maneuver around corners and through doorways. Especially hard is pushing the wheelchair up a ramp, and then holding it when it goes back down again.

They have financial assistance with governmental and insurance aid; however, there are so many unexpected expenses. Changes in their lifestyle and major adjustments have caused a continual drain on their retirement savings. Martha does the budgeting since her husband's stroke; and the way she figures it, they will run out of savings next year.

As the church people walk by Mary, Martha and Martha's husband, they greet them with "How are you? It's good to see you. Haven't seen you in a while." Some even add, "Can I help you up the ramp? You don't look well today. Is anything wrong?" Some may venture to stop and even look them in the face during conversation. Others sit next to them during the service.

What a wonderful opportunity for the church to minister! Few suffer in our society like the abused or handicapped—those unfortunate persons battered by life or illness. They live with pain every hour of every day. Even when they find some physical relief, their mind works on them with thoughts of anger, guilt or escape.

The church only responds to them before, during and after the church service. A few congregations work outside of the church service, spending a Saturday building a ramp to a person's porch or making a telephone call to see how someone is feeling. A small number of other churches may have a ministry expressly for the abused or the handicapped, but the opportunities to minister greatly increase as the climax of the church week begins.

Meanwhile, the congregation turns away from those nearby and looks toward the front, the stage. Watching the people in front of them, they view the church at its best—the best music, the best presentation and the best preaching. Even Mary is looking at what the church sees. Martha, however, is still trying to get her husband in just the right position, and keep him from blocking someone else's view.

The sermon that day is about the virtues of discipleship, how the Christian has left the pathways of sin to traverse the highway to a better life. "Only believe" is the theme echoed by the preacher. "Turn your troubles into triumphs" is the anthem chanted and repeated from pulpit to pew. "We're a church moving to the next level," "We've left the sorrows of Egypt behind," and "We are on the King's highway," are the points emphasized in the sermon.

A few minutes later Mary, Martha and her husband realize they are not included in the sermon at all. It is not for sinners, it is for those who have come out of sin and for those struggling to have faith. The sermon does not cover the abused, the elderly or the handicapped. One might say the sermon does refer to them indirectly. But explain to Mary, Martha and her husband who live moment-by-moment with their pain how the message touches them indirectly.

The truth is, neither the preacher nor the sermon is targeting these three souls waiting in the pew. The message is for people like the preacher and others the church has collected. It's for people wanting to get ahead in life, to get over their past failures or to improve the spiritual disciplines in their life. It is not for people who just want to get through the next hour without caving in to the pain. It is not for those who yearn for an evening without yelling and the unpredictable mayhem from an angry spouse, or those who wonder what can stop them from the giant skid toward poverty brought on by age, illness and the inability to work.

What Do Believers See?

A look around many churches today reveals a group of people doing reasonably well. They have illness in their family; but mainly, those who continually suffer do not go to their churches. The suffering members of the families stopped coming years ago. So did other friends and people who messed up their lives with sinful follies of adultery, drugs or foolish activity. The people in church are hard-working people who believe in God.

Thank the Lord, they do come to church and they do love the Lord. The problem is that the church may become accustomed to seeing a world and a church only made up of hard-working, successful people. They may have forgotten about the hurting, the abused, the impoverished, the ill and the handicapped. There are not fewer handicapped, abused or dying people in the world; they just are not coming to church.

Do not think that they can't come; they are choosing not to come to church. They do not come because church is not made for them anymore. It once was. The church was originally designed by the Lord to be a haven and a refuge. It was meant to be the very place where people could find comfort and rest. It was not meant to be a gathering place of just people doing well and looking to improve their lives . . . or only people climbing higher mountains of faith . . . or people who only want to raise their families. The church was birthed by the blood of Christ for all the people we see in church and all the ones who have stopped coming to church.

If the average churchgoer were to profile the person who does not attend church, what would he or she look like? The church attender may see the person as a sinner in need of salvation, a sinner who needs to live a holy life, or a sinner who is just too irresponsible to come to church. In reality, the person is more than just a sinner who needs to be saved by grace.

The key to reaching the sinners in your church is not just the redemption of their sins, but it involves all of the other things they carry with them—pain, suffering and poverty. They carry abuse from a father who was supposed to protect them. They carry a physical condition brought on by an illness they did not ask for. They certainly cannot forget about the poverty they live in that was brought on by generations of wrong choices and crippling addictions.

How would Jesus profile the person who is not attending your church?

Can We See Jesus Hurting?

How we view the person not going to church depends on how we see Jesus. What does the Savior look like to church people? Little is said today about the Jesus men and women were acquainted with while He was on the earth. The descriptions in Scripture are of a young boy, dependent on His parents; of a man who was found among the poor, the sick, the demon-possessed and sinners; and a man that many did not want to look at. He was known for His successes, but ultimately marked by what many called failure. He was rejected by popular opinion and even despised. He was given little chance of leaving a lasting impression, dying between convicted criminals in an act of capital punishment. His last words on earth were uttered from the depths of His pain and separation from His Father.

Oh yes, there are glorious descriptions of Christ, the Christ of victory. Those descriptions, however, are of Christ after His earthly life was over. He is the King, but His throne room was revealed to us only after He suffered. When believers are told in Hebrews 12:1-3 to receive faith from Christ by looking on Him, the image we are given is Christ hanging on the cross. Not once in chapter 11's descriptions of faith are we shown the Christ of glory.

To know Christ in the "power of His resurrection," Paul explained in Philippians 3:10, one has to know Christ in the "fellowship of His sufferings." The word *fellowship* implies we have to embrace His suffering. Just as a person would thoroughly fellowship with Christ through prayer, fasting and Bible reading, so an individual grows closer to His suffering on the cross by suffering with Him. Pain would then be no stranger, isolation no foreigner and suffering would not be alien.

Paul does not mean that one should physically hurt

himself or herself. The believer is not to disdain suffering as though it is not part of the Christian life. The
believer is not to avoid those who are suffering as
though they are less spiritual. The believer is not to
reject those wounded in life as though they have done
something wrong. Drawn to the suffering, the believer must minister to them just as Christ used suffering
as a gateway to minister to others.

What Is Your Picture of Christ?

Isaiah illustrates the suffering Christ graphically in
chapters 52 and 53 of his prophecy. Today, Christ is
a success in the business world, always a powerful
warrior and ever a miracle worker who walks on the
water to meet any of our requests. Isaiah breaks into
our range of vision with a much different Christ.
Isaiah 52:13 says "Behold, My Servant shall . . . be
exalted and extolled and be very high." That's wor-
thy of a king. But when we see the exalted One in the
passage, He is unlike any king we have ever seen.
The next two verses tell us what the exalted One
looks like:

> Just as many were astonished at you, so His visage
> was marred more than any man, and His form more
> than the sons of men; so shall He sprinkle many
> nations. Kings shall shut their mouths at Him; for
> what had not been told them they shall see, and what
> they had not heard they shall consider (vv. 14, 15).

Kings would be appalled because they were made
to look at Him. The people expected a king like the
kings on earth — dressed in fine linen, robes and all the
trappings of power. The next few verses in Isaiah con-

tinue to describe him as One who was suffering, despised and rejected by others:

> Who has believed our report? And to whom has the arm of the Lord been revealed? For He shall grow up before Him as a tender plant, and as a root out of dry ground. He has no form or comeliness; and when we see Him, there is no beauty that we should desire Him. He is despised and rejected by men, a Man of sorrows and acquainted with grief. And we hid, as it were, our faces from Him; He was despised, and we did not esteem Him. Surely He has borne our griefs and carried our sorrows; yet we esteemed Him stricken, smitten by God, and afflicted. But He was wounded for our transgressions, He was bruised for our iniquities; the chastisement for our peace was upon Him, and by His stripes we are healed (53:1-5).

Notice that Christ was not viewed as a powerful warrior riding the clouds of glory and returning to earth as He is depicted in the Book of Revelation. Rather, He is the Healer on earth who was wounded in order to make the relief of our sorrows possible. He comes to those He has identified with and ministered to them.

In the same way, the contemporary Christian's call to care is not just a matter of helping people get better. Rather, it is the necessity of nurturing a personal empathy for the needy and their sufferings. We must be "acquainted with grief," which is more than merely helping the grieving. When we bond with the hurting, our care becomes more than an act of service; it becomes a ministry.

The descriptions of the reaction of the people of

God to Jesus and His appearance is powerful. The people of God rejected, despised and turned away from the suffering Savior. His suffering and apparent weakness in comparison to the power of kings and health of the strong was the reason they could not embrace Him. In the same way, Christ comes to the modern church in the form of the poor, the downcast, the handicapped and the abused of the world.

Matthew 25:31-46 describes the judgment of Christ. At that time, Christ will inform each person passing by Him that He was on earth, giving them an opportunity to reach out to Him. He was there as the poor, the weak and the needy. Sadly, many will be rejected at the Judgment because they did not embrace Him by ministering to the broken, the battered and the bruised.

Is There Value in Caring for the Hurting?

The examples the church follows are often the opposite of the examples Christ left us. Rather than following the One who went to the oppressed, we elevate the overcomer. Instead of following Him to the afflicted, we rush to the unaffected. When we should follow Christ to the prisoner, we parade the privileged. We have it all backwards.

We are overcomers when we stand with the oppressed. We are immune from the "diseases of Egypt" (see Exodus 15:26) when we sit with the afflicted. We are set free when we go to the prisoner. We have the riches of Christ when we give of ourselves to the poor. We have the mind of Christ when we respond to the question of Isaiah 53:8, "Who will declare His generation?" by becoming a generation "acquainted with grief" as He was.

Besides developing a guiding vision for care (ch. 2), one of the strategic steps for a church to take is to list its core values. Core values are the most important ones held by the church. They may not be the only values of the church, but they are the most critical to the life and meaning of the local body. Core values are not developed overnight; they are not the product of a late-night meeting of a single board or committee.

Core values are actually the reflection of the existing values of the church. They also include the values to which the church would like to aspire. Values in the church incorporate those priorities the church is currently developing. Displaying its foremost ideals, the core values of a church state clearly and consistently what the church holds most dear. The church should publicly declare that it considers the bonds the church has with the broken, the poor and the hurting of the church and community as the very foundation of its ministry.

Ministry is more than a highway to credibility for the church. Caring for the ill, the handicapped and the elderly is more than just part of a punch list for holiness. Meeting the needs of the impoverished is not just another line item on the church budget. The caring church identifies with the despised, the rejected and the poor. Service is who the church is, not just an act. Bonding with the needy, the church must reach within itself and beyond itself to actually bear and absorb the pains, sufferings and griefs of those in need. Christ himself agonized with those He reached — He actually gave His life for them! A church's very existence is dependent on how it cares.

How Can the Church Minister With Care?

Can we tolerate the suffering of those who are not yet delivered? Does the church see itself as invincible or able to absorb pain? Is tragedy a word often spoken but *heard* much less in our worship?

Look at Mary, Martha and Martha's husband. The congregation rises at the end of the sermon, and a woman walks up the aisle. The people have their heads bowed in meditation at the request of the pastor, and a believer named Sarah moves next to Mary. Mary looks up and sees tears streaming down Sarah's face. Sarah has read the story in Mary's eyes; she knows why Mary's clothes are long—they are hiding her bruises. Sarah too has fought with a husband blinded by rage. She remembers what it was like to hear her children screaming for the mayhem to stop.

Rather than hiding, Sarah is reaching out and touching the broken places in Mary's heart. For the first time since the service began, Mary begins to receive from the church.

Meanwhile, Martha has struggled to stand. The minutes during the sermon is one of the longest periods of uninterrupted rest she has had all week. There is a movement, and she looks to her left. Amazingly, three men, old friends of her husband's, have come to pray with him. One leans over to embrace him. The others have their eyes closed, their hands lifted and their hearts opened heavenward as they continue to pray. These old fishing buddies have discovered that friendship in church is more than just a meal after church and a men's activity on Saturday.

What made Sarah move across the aisle?

What made three friends walk across the church to a fallen comrade?

When we see Christ, we notice those who are hurting. When Christ is in full view, we notice those who are broken. When the fellowship of the Cross is embraced, we pay attention to the poor. A church that looks on the body of our Lord becomes a broken church, and a broken church is ready to minister.

STRATEGIC TRANSFORMATION STEP
Develop a list of core values that emphasize the central role of care.

PROCEDURE TO DEVELOP
Make care a central priority of each local church ministry.

IMPLICATIONS FOR CARE
The church becomes a caring church rather than just a church that cares.

4
THE GENERATION OF THE WOUNDED HEALER

W hen the church has no system for caring, the body is without wholeness. The needy hear only words and never experience actions. While the members of the body can become disjointed and dislocated, care is the sinew that holds the various parts together. No matter how strong the parts of the system of the church are, no matter how gifted individuals may be, with no planned venue for care and compassion, the body is dysfunctional and dismembered. Feelings and sentimentality must be turned into structure. Care must be structured so that it is connected with every person in the church.

The Search for a Home

Walk through the business district of an average metropolis, across the parkway from the arts district, and you'll meet Ed. If you stop to admire the gleaming skyscrapers and the busy commuters, you probably won't see him. If you are thinking too long about the banks and the businesses, you'll walk right past him. But go past the department store windows with their displays of next season's fashions, around the corner and down an alley, and you'll find Ed's home on the other side of the dumpsters.

Ed is busy most of the day, trying to scrape out an existence. It comes mainly from the rear doors of restaurants, shops and offices. He searches for food and items left over because no one else wanted them. He carries a sack, and pushes a cart from time to time. During winter months, he spends most of his time trying to stay warm. He can usually find a little heat and warmth among his friends as they huddle together against a wall.

He didn't always live on Second Street—just two blocks from Main. He used to live 12 blocks over on 14th Street—on the other side of the Interstate. He had put a few things together—boxes, boards and a couple of cushions—and spent the summer there. Then he was evicted from the lot when a business began clearing for a new convenience store. Several years ago Ed lived in another part of the state. In fact, he used to have a house that was his home, not just a place to stay.

When you see him, you might see that he looks as if he has been hungry for a long time. He has lived on the street for about five years. Although he tries to straighten himself up once in a while, he can't remember the last time he really cleaned up. He attended college when he was younger, but the past five years have given him his most intensive education. He could tell us a lot.

Ed is a survivor. He observes people. He likes to talk—and does, every chance he gets. When he feels like it, he goes to a mission church services. He's had a lot of experience with church and family. Ed was once an elder on a church council. In fact, he was the chief elder. Married, with four children, he was the store manager at a local department store in the small city where he lived.

Perhaps you know someone like Ed, or maybe you just know about the homeless. He may or may not have fallen on hard times. For sure he made a lot of wrong choices. He sinned against the Lord and walked away from his family. He was hit by a difficult illness that year, but he was recovering. Things were going well on his job. Actually Ed himself is mostly responsible for living the way he does now. Do you know Ed?

Bringing Care Home

Everyone knows about the homeless. They are defined as a group in society without a house, an apartment or a place to live. They wander in cities and in rural America. They live outdoors mostly— under highway overpasses, in alleys and in temporary community shelters. They have no money and no food. They move through our roads, villages, towns, cities and highways, primarily unnoticed until certain times of the year.

For some people, Thanksgiving is more meaningful if they help feed the homeless. Other holidays stir remembrance of the less fortunate. Some make feeding the homeless a regular, weekly or even daily part of their lives. A heroic few have dedicated their lives to caring for the homeless.

Meanwhile, back at the church on the corner. Even if the church feeds the needy every day, how many saints within the church have a place in their hearts for those with nowhere to live? Few churches do more than give the homeless a passing thought between holidays. Even in churches that benevolently reach the less fortunate, the fabric of the church is not significantly sewn with a ministry of care to those who are on the outside looking in.

The irony is that if you ask the average churchgoer, "Do you care about those in society who are without—without food, without shelter, without clothing?" the resounding, sincere answer will be, "Yes!" It will be a sincere answer, uttered from pure hearts. But what causes the compassion within that answer to leave the homeless wandering outside? What drags like an anchor on the spiritual bottom of most churches to keep them from moving? What will propel a church past intentions, all the way to intervention?

A church gives only what it possesses. The problem of reaching the homeless must begin with reaching the abandoned within the church. Ironically, many of the homeless in the church would tell you they have a home. Yet, many will tell you that they do not feel at home in their churches. Many homeless people on the streets, without four walls and a roof over their heads, feel more of a sense of home than people who have the walls, the roof, the heat, the air-conditioning and plenty of food on the table. It may be that the church does not reach out more to the needy because it has not yet learned how to meet its own needs.

The message of this book is still about caring for the searching, the hurting and the hungry. The focus will not suddenly change and zero in on the church ministering to itself. But what message does the church have to give to the homeless if empty, hopeless and homeless people are found within the local body of believers? What gifts can they bring, what difference can they make, when persons who attend do not feel that the church is a home and a haven for them? Reaching one group is directly related to reaching the other.

How well you know the suffering and hurting determines how well you will minister to them—both inside and outside the church. How well do you know the homeless in your church? Sporadic attendance, occasional participation and lack of enthusiasm may indicate that they feel like outsiders, although they have attended the church for years. You may say, "They need to become more involved," "They only get out of church what they put in," or "They know we're here for them," but the fact remains that many in our sanctuaries feel they have been left on the outside.

Love for the Homeless Begins at Home

Ministry is an extension of the condition of the church. A church ministers out of the riches of its relationship with Christ. A church also ministers out of the relationship of its members to each other. Proclaiming Christ was never intended by the heavenly Father to be something that only He does. It is not merely something people in the church do as individuals. A Christian's personal walk with the Lord may be wonderful, but ministry is not something done by individuals in isolation from others in the church. The greatest battles of ministry are won by an army of believers, not by individuals.

A church is not fully ministering if the activities of ministry representing that local body are only done by a handful of people. Ministry flows from fellowship; care is created by community. Help comes from the church home of the family of God. Christ ministered first to His disciples, then to the crowds around them. He did not stop for the blind before he instructed the men who followed Him. Christ led the disciples, conversing with them, eating with them, resting with them and experiencing life with them. They felt at home with the Master; they didn't just show up for a meeting once a week.

Love for one another in the fellowship of the church is a great rehearsal for loving the world. Many in the church today have not even shown up for practice. The pastor works on the stage, the council prints the tickets and faithful workers print programs. But when it comes time to perform, there is no play or production. The church has skirted around the issue of loving one another, and as a result it is not prepared for offering love and care to the world.

Your House

Isaiah 58 exploded into the consciousness of the people of Judah.

> Cry aloud, spare not; lift up your voice like a trumpet; tell My people their transgression, and the house of Jacob their sins. Yet they seek Me daily, and delight to know My ways, as a nation that did righteousness, and did not forsake the ordinance of their God. They ask of Me the ordinances of justice; they take delight in approaching God (vv. 1, 2).

Through the prophet, the Lord demanded that the message be cried out and nothing held back. Taking notice of what they did, He identified their many activities. Their busyness was an investment in good things. They sought God daily, they delighted to know His ways, they were a righteous nation, and they were faithful to God's ordinances. They sought justice and enjoyed doing all those things willingly.

But like a verdict falling on a defendant's ears in a court room, verses 3-5 unmasks their pleasurable religion and reveals their lack of love. They were cautious in their pursuit of God, scrambling only to the places that were convenient. The Lord told them they only wanted to serve Him when it was pleasurable, and that they measured every ounce of their investment, making sure it wouldn't cost them too much (see v. 3). As a result, God did not answer their petitions. Their cries were personal requests — not prayers for ministry.

God told them that truly serving Him meant that those in bondage would be released, those under a heavy burden would be relieved and the oppressed would be delivered (v. 6). They had religion, but they did not have a relationship. They prayed, had church and were a righteous nation; but they withheld themselves from unrestrained caring. They did not reach out to others in the household of faith, and lacked the dimension of ministering to one another. They measured their religion by how far it required them to go past individual pleasures and securities. They wanted to receive personally, not noticing those in the next pew who were without.

The Lord addressed their failure to reach one another by challenging them to personally take the first step to reach out. He challenged their personal involvement by asking if truly serving Him meant "that you break every yoke? Is it not to share your bread with the hungry, and that you bring to your house the poor who are cast out; when you see the naked, that you cover him, and not hide yourself from your own flesh? (vv. 6, 7).

The Lord did not say, "Make sure the hungry are fed." That would have been good, but He went further. He said to feed the hungry yourself. He did not say just make sure the poor receive help, He said to bring the poor into your own house. They were to cover the naked, not let someone else do it. The Lord's major concern was their personal involvement in the needs and lives of those they met. He wanted them to take personal notice of the condition of those around them.

You may think the Lord was speaking about ministry to the people outside of Judah. However, he summarized their work by telling them to "not hide yourself from your own flesh" (v. 7). They had failed to even take care of themselves. Because they failed to properly care for others, they neglected themselves. They had deceived themselves into thinking that protecting themselves and commending themselves would improve them. To the contrary, care for others is the means God has selected for healthy self-esteem and genuine personal development. Christians who withhold themselves from others are like a stream that has become stagnant. Jesus said, "Whoever desires to save his life will lose it, but whoever loses his life for My sake will find it" (Matthew 16:25).

Of even deeper interest was His use of the word *house* in Isaiah 58:7. God did not answer their prayers, because they were not answering the cries of their own brothers and sisters. Judah did not receive, because the people did not give to each other. They gave themselves to many religious activities, but they did not give themselves to the needs of each other. God was speaking to a nation that He wanted to be a family.

In the same way, the care for one another in the church should be as thick as the blood of Christ that flows within His church. God was demanding that the people of Judah minister to each other as a family—take care of each other. Their care was to have been first to one another, then to the world. God demands that the church today prepare to reach the homeless lying on the street corners by first reaching each other in the body of Christ.

Work and Care Together

Those searching for a caring church want to see care demonstrated within the church. The church may advertise care, talk care and even do acts of care for its visitors. The searching soul, however, needs to see care in action among the people of God. The visitor is asking, "Do I want to be a part of a church that treats its own people this way?"

Picture someone who is kind to everyone else but has little time for his or her own family. You would have a hard time believing the sincerity or integrity of that person. If you were asked whether you wanted to join that person in mutual activity, you would have second thoughts. In the same way, guests in your church want to identify with a group that supports each other, holds up each other and genuinely knows each other.

A strategic step for a church is to approach ministry from a team or group perspective. Rather than just equipping individuals to do the work of the Lord, equip people to work together, with and for each other. There is power in unity and solidarity. God promised He would "command" His blessing where unity was found among His people (see Psalm 133).

In addition to developing a guiding vision (ch. 2) and listing its most critical values (ch. 3), a church can move toward transformation and become a caring church by equipping its people to minister together. The skills to learn are love, patience, longsuffering, forgiveness and care for each other—even before we learn bricklaying, teaching techniques or witnessing programs.

Meetings must begin with sensitivity and prayer for one another before there are project reports. Members should see each other informally, outside of church, just because they care for each other. They should ask about each other's family, and share about how things are going at work. They even need to have fun together, much as Jesus must have when He lived and walked with His family of 12 disciples.

Going Home With Ed

Maybe Ed's story could have been different if his church had noticed he was headed for trouble. Truth is, they respected him because he was the chief elder, but most of the church people really didn't know him. He had become very good at being a church member and ministry leader, but not very good at caring. Part of the tragedy was that his local church allowed it to happen. He was helpful and a great blessing, and he made a difference in his church and community. Sadly, he was everything a church attender should be except to be himself, knowing others in the church and allowing others to know and care for him.

The church people didn't really know Ed, because he didn't let others care for him. Consequently, he never noticed that he didn't care for others. He led the council and church, assisting the pastor in many other ministries, but no one noticed his slide into confusion, pain and eventually sin. It was private.

Ed is still unnoticed today. His church did not provide a home for him years ago, and neither does the church provide one for him today. Caring for the world is just an extension of the local church's care for one another.

STRATEGIC TRANSFORMATION STEP
Develop effective team-building skills for the local body.

PROCEDURE TO DEVELOP
Prioritize care for one another as the heart of the ministry agenda.

IMPLICATIONS FOR CARE
Care for the hurting world becomes an extension of care within the body.

—————5—————
THE FALLEN,
THE FAILING AND
THE FORGIVEN

Today's church only sees itself as consisting of successful people, and its tolerance for failure is low. Its desire and passion are not expressed in care, but in the careers of its members. In greater numbers, the fallen of society and the failed within the church no longer look to the church for comfort. An awareness of this failure is necessary for spiritual success in any church.

Care cannot be an option, an occasion for the church to shine. Care cannot be merely another priority among many others; it must be the first priority, reaching both the fallen and those who reside on the mountains of success.

Description of a Fall

Caring for Bob is difficult. He once held such promise, but now he doesn't promise much of anything. Everything he touches seems to fall apart. He once would walk into church and catch everyone's attention. He was young, full of promise and had his life under control. From high school, he went to college. After graduation he landed a good job and worked for one of the most successful firms in town.

He had always been a good kid. His parents were proud of him. People had watched him grow up in church. He was an example to everyone around him. Bob even had a storybook marriage. His wife was a Christian, and they were involved in church. They had their first child during the second year of marriage. The family moved into a new home in the best part of town. They were an example for other families to follow. Any church would feel blessed to have them.

They hadn't been in their new home long before Bob began to change. He was irritable at home and out in public. People began to notice the change. He wasn't seen around church functions as much. His wife continued attending with the baby, but Bob didn't. Then his wife began to cry during the church services.

When Bob did come, he seemed untouched by anything that happened in the services. The pastor talked with Bob, trying to see if he would respond and open up. Some of Bob's friends at church tried to talk with him, but it was to no avail. Bob was shut up tight. He quit going out with any of the church people, leaving everyone wondering what was going on.

Bob began taking regular excursions every night. To do this, all he only had to sit at his desk and turn on the computer. Slowly, night after night, unknown to his wife or anyone that knew him, he began to slide deeper and deeper into the evils of the Web. Just as a spider's web entraps its victims, the World Wide Web computer network can become a trap. Bob was an expert in Internet communications and with computers in general. His computer skills and use of the Web was one of his strengths on the job. He was able to maneuver his way carefully through the Web, hiding his moves from the view of even the most adept computer user.

No one else knew the private battle unfolding in Bob's life. It started with curious inquiries when he and his wife were in their old home. Things weren't going too well between them, and Bob began to view pornographic sites. As the months went by, Bob appeared to be the same on the outside. Inwardly, however, Bob began to live an alternative lifestyle on the Web. He chose different names when communicating on the various sites. He joined pornographic chat rooms. He "met" other pornography users on the computer. Gradually, his sin on the Web changed who he was on the outside.

Bob sank deeply into a quicksand of deceit. He deceived others, but he himself was the one most deceived. He convinced himself that his covert life of sexual promiscuity was justified. He felt hurt and rejected by his friends, his family and his wife. He began having secret meetings with his Web "friends." He started to commit adultery with different women.

In the meantime, his addiction to pornography was becoming more and more open. His wife made the first discovery when she saw some pictures and notices left behind by the computer. Friends began to see his language and topics of conversation change. Finally, he told his wife he wanted to live in open sexual promiscuity, and that he felt there was nothing wrong with adultery.

The irony was that Bob would still talk to the pastor and others at church. They were his lifelong friends and companions, but he thought his personal business was his own concern. He would talk about anything except his addiction. He didn't even call it an addiction; he just wouldn't talk about it at all. Internet pornography, illicit chat rooms and sexual liaisons began to control his life. He felt he could work out his own marriage; and he wanted to continue to have his job, his social standing and his church. Ironically, Bob had hardened his heart and justified his extra-marital affairs.

The Crossroads of Care

The local church is at a crossroads. How do you care for the habitual sinner without condoning his or her sin? The sin is real; there is no theological question about Bob's sinfulness. But what do you do with Bob? He hasn't left his wife. He hasn't left the church. He feels justified in his mind, but he is wrong. Nevertheless, the church must respond to this success turned failure. Bob once represented all of the best virtues of the church; now, he is a reminder of a Christian's spiritual failure. How will the church deal with this failure?

The church not only has to deal with moral failure, but also with other failures within the church. People attend who are failures on their jobs. Sometimes it is their fault; at other times they have just fallen on hard times. Young people fail in school. Many do not make the academic honor roll and have trouble passing their classes. People fail to live healthy lives — they do not take care of their physical bodies. Some are social failures, awkward around others and an embarrassment by the way they act.

Still others struggle with an up-and-down spiritual life. They try to get better. They recover temporarily from a life of sin, and then slip back into old lifestyles and habits. The congregation sees them in and out of church, as they go back and forth to the altar. They've been through various discipleship programs. Some demonstrate amazing progress, only to fall back into what seems like worse conditions. Then they return to the Lord again.

At some point, the frustration level rises for many in the church. Successes are something a church can testify about, but what do you do with perpetual failure? How many times does a church have to see a person stumble, seemingly never getting any better? They remind the church that their prayers are still unanswered. They tell the church that sin can return to a person's life. A parade of unsuccessful people walk into church every week.

There are people in the church who remain sick for long periods of time. They have unsightly or inconvenient conditions that demand a lot of attention. They cause people to shake their heads in disbelief, wondering if they will ever get any better. They have conditions of the mind and body that are hard to understand. They are unable to do things,

and they have behaviors that some of the people in
the church cannot understand.

Church people respond to this dilemma in a vari-
ety of personal and theological ways. Some church-
goers only see that sinners reap the consequences of
their sins and confuse consequences with possible
sins. They wonder whether some of these individuals fail in life because of a hidden sin. Others in the
church feel that some people remain in trouble
because of a lack of faith. Still others choose to ignore
the failures in the church, only concentrating on and
befriending successful people.

Does this sound a little hard on churchgoing folk?
Does it sound as if the church may be callous or
insensitive to spiritual, economic, physical or social
failings? Then ask yourself these questions.

- Can a person in our church fail and still come
  to church?

- Can a person in our church fail and no one in
  the church know about it?

- Will the ministries of the church be successful
  enough to encompass the fallen?

- How spiritual are we?

- How many have we restored?

Caring for Failures

What should be the church's response to the failures of Christians? Whether the condition of the person is directly related to some personal sin or not,

what should be the response? Essentially, the call of Scripture is to restore the fallen within the church. This does not mean sin should be excused; it means the church should be committed to ministering to them. The church should endeavor to restore them, even for an extended period of time. The church should also endeavor to restore those who were once in church but have stopped coming. Finally, restoration is the goal for those who never even came to our church.

Restoration is a difficult part of care. It involves a lot of commitment and a lot of patience. The supreme example of restoration is found in the heavenly Father's faithful love. Long after we lose the endurance to continually hope for the recovery of those who repeatedly fall, the Father's love still reaches out to them. Christ's purpose was to seek and save the lost, to go after other sheep outside the fold (John 10:16). The effort to bring back a stray lamb means that the ministering shepherd goes after the lost one, encountering personal danger, hazardous conditions and life-threatening perils (see John 10:10-15). The ministering shepherd not only reflects Christ's ministry, but also represents pastors and caring believers within the church.

The Biblical Mandate of Restoration

Matthew 18 describes the lengths to which the church should go to reach and restore failures. The disciples were at odds with one another, arguing about who was the greatest in the kingdom (v. 1). Jesus responded by warning them that they were to treat each other with care, as if they were tender children (vv. 2-14). Then Jesus describes what they were to do if a brother or sister in the church fails (vv. 15-20).

Have you ever had a personal trespass of some kind against you? It may have been a sin or an indiscretion committed against you. The offender may have been your spouse or someone close; it may have been someone you did not know. This lesson of Jesus applies to those times when another person has failed in the Christian life.

Jesus' instruction to you is to go to the person and endeavor to restore the individual (v. 15). If you are unable to restore him or her, you are to enlist others in the church to help you (v. 16). If one or two of you are unable to restore the offender, you are to get more help from the church (v. 17). Ultimately, you may not be able to restore the person.

Restoration and forgiveness are synonymous in this passage. Forgiveness is the initial act that starts the longer process of restoration. Peter asked how many times we are to restore or forgive the person (v. 21). Jesus replied that forgiveness and restoration are to continue, even when the person fails to respond and turn away from his or her sin and failure (vv. 22-35).

The role of restoration was accentuated by Christ in Matthew 18. He gave three Scriptural exhortations that have been used by believers to refer to power in prayer and attending church. The context of these passages, however, was restoration. In verse 18, Christ said that their ability to restore affected their ability to intercede for the binding and freeing of spiritual things. In verse 19, He emphasized that seeking restoration and agreement among themselves was related to the Father answering their prayers. In verse 20, He reminded them that meeting together in the name of the Lord with those in need affected the presence of the Lord in their midst.

Paul also taught about the need for restoration. In Galatians 5:16–6:1, he wrote about the lust of the flesh and the corresponding works that follow. He went on to cite the work of the Spirit that produces fruit in the life of the believer. He only listed one outward work of the Spirit, however. Without a doubt, outward works result from the inward work of the Spirit and the fruit of the Spirit. Paul only listed one, however, highlighting its importance. The outward work he listed was the restoration of the failing and the fallen (6:1). Essentially, Paul asked the church to measure its spirituality, in large part, by the number of people it had restored.

Targeting the Fallen and the Failing

In addition to developing a guiding vision (ch. 2), listing its most critical values (ch. 3) and transforming into a caring church by equipping its people to minister together (ch. 4), a church can determine who it will reach. A church with a vision, values and ministry teams needs to accurately target who it would like to reach with its ministries. Assess target groups in the community, as well as those within your body of believers. Both need ministry. Profiling these groups can help the church design caring ministries. The church may want to reach special population groups identified by ethnicity, culture, financial status, educational level, vocation, family status or many other variables.

One variable that identifies the lost and hurting is failure. Much of the pain they experience is the result of some kind of failure. The failure may be something for which they are responsible. At other times they may experience failure through no fault of their own. In both cases, the failure is real and the resulting needs are real. The church's persistence in restoring the failing and the hurting should target those who respond and those who do not.

Some may even be resistant, insisting on persisting in their failures and/or fallen state. Whether they respond or not, the church must try to restore.

Restoring Bob

As the church continues to minister to Bob, it must be prepared for setbacks. Call Bob a member of the *70 x 7 Club*—those people who fit the category referred to by Jesus in Matthew 18:22. Peter asked Jesus how many times he must forgive and restore the trespasser, and Jesus told him to do it 70 x 7 times. Jesus meant that the work must continue, regardless of the continued trespass and failings of the other person. The church's goal with Bob is not to continue to work with him until he asks the Lord for forgiveness and lives the Christian life successfully. Rather, the church is to continue with compassion (see v. 27), regardless of whether Bob responds.

Situations like Bob's may get harder before they get better. Bob may stop contributing to the church. He may create bigger problems for his wife. He may become more and more irresponsible. He may even lose his job, because he is so changed by his new lifestyle. Is Bob on the fringe, or at the heart of ministry? He is a draining person; he will not contribute like he once did, or the way others do in the church.

The church has a few decisions to make. Can a church build its ministry around people like Bob who still come to church but have constant problems? What if Bob's problem was poverty, disease or illness, instead of pornography? What if his problem was laziness or irresponsibility? What if Bob was on the fringe of homelessness?

Can a church build its ministry around extremely draining people? The answer is yes. A church builds its 70 x 7 ministry around the people Peter asked about in Matthew 18. A church cannot build its ministering team, its leadership, its financial base or its structure of support around Bob; but its ministry should be targeted on the Bobs of the world.

Struggling souls have fallen overboard the ship of God's safety, His church. They are desperately trying to make it on the sea of life. It is impossible for them to pull themselves back on board. They still swim near the ship, so there is still hope. Christ, the great Captain, pilots the ship. He has seen them fall. He sees the struggles of the fallen; He knows their up-and-down disappointments, as well as those of their relatives on board. His strong arm is ready to pull them to safety.

But He has designed His church in such a way that those on board are the lifeline that reaches the lost, connecting them to His saving arm. Look around you. Has anyone looked overboard for those who keep falling off the ship? Some may say, "We've pulled them out so many times? How many times do we have to do this?" The fact is, no matter how many times they have fallen, they will never get back on board until we reach them and restore them to the arm of the Savior.

STRATEGIC TRANSFORMATION STEP
Identify target groups to be reached by the varied ministries in the church.

PROCEDURE TO DEVELOP
Commit to reaching each group regardless of the success or failure.

IMPLICATIONS FOR CARE
Reconciling needy people who are hurting results from walking in the Spirit.

6
LEARNING TO FOLLOW IN ORDER TO LEAD

A church must be Spirit-led if it is to be a caring church. Most believers' problems today stem from the fact that the church leads itself instead of relying on the leadership of the Spirit. Rather than finding where the Spirit is leading and following that path, we make our plans and then ask the Spirit to lead. The church simply must become better at following the path of the Spirit.

The path of the leading of the Spirit begins at the crossroads of care. Understand that care, ultimately, is prompted and sustained by divine leadership, rather than human. The Holy Spirit gives constant care to those inside and outside the church. The nature of the Holy Spirit is to be present with us, right where and when we are in need, leading us in the care process.

The Holy Spirit Makes It Possible

Jim was amazed. The church service seemed to

flow like the gentle run of a river. The pastor seemed to notice what Jim really needed and felt. Jim was stirred because it had been a long time since he had felt such a spiritual and personal connection in a church service. He had come with a burden for his parents. They were both in desperate financial need. The soloist that morning gave a testimony about her family and how God had met their needs. Jim did not know what had prompted the church to know so well just what he needed that morning. Only God could have allowed total strangers to know how to touch him so deeply.

Sandy works on the same job day after day, week after week. She likes her job, but it can become monotonous. She is raising two children on her own. Since her divorce eight years ago, she has had to make a living for herself and her children. It has been a tall order, giving little time to waste during the day. Her weekends are filled with catching up on visits to the doctor's office, buying groceries and a seemingly endless list of things to do. In fact, weekends are more hectic than the workweeks. She winds down to go to work on Monday morning.

The best part of each workday is her lunch hour when she meets with her friend, Betty. Every day, Monday through Friday, noon is Sandy's favorite hour. It is the only retreat she has from her busy schedule as a single, working mom. It is the only time she can make a choice that is hers and hers alone. It is the only time she can talk to someone about her own needs and wants. Betty listens. In fact, it is uncanny how well Betty listens. She seems to know just what to say to make Sandy feel better. She has the patience and the time to build up Sandy daily. Betty speaks to Sandy about church and about serving God. She has not convinced Sandy to do it yet, but Sandy feels comfortable listening to Betty, because Betty is there for her.

Frank has worked for his company many years. He is one of the hardest workers in the whole plant, and he minds his own business. He has seen the best and the worst of a lot of people on the job. Many have come and gone, but he has survived them all. Through the years, he has noticed Harry, a man who has been at the plant nearly as long as Frank. Frank notices something genuine and different about Harry.

Frank cannot remember Harry ever flying off the handle or getting out of control. Harry has helped a lot of guys at the plant, doing extra work to help the men out. Frank admires him for that. Harry is one of the few men, besides the supervisors, who speaks to Frank. Harry has even invited him to church. Frank almost went one year, but that was the year his daughter was in an automobile accident. Harry went to the hospital to visit her three times that week. He prayed with her and asked his pastor to come by.

Three different people—Jim, Sandy and Frank— had the same experience. All three knew people from the church down the street. They found these people to be special, because they listened and took time to share with others. They were genuinely kind and caring. They reached out to others and helped them when they were in need.

All three were touched by the sensitivity of these Christians. The believers seemed to know just what

it would take to help others. They were not too
pushy and or too religious. They shared the message
of Christ with sensitivity and openness, accurately
applying words of comfort at the time it counted
most. Those believers not only ministered to others
in church, but also to their friends, neighbors and
coworkers with care and compassion.

Does this picture sound too good to be true? People
from a local church sharing with others in and out of
church? Does it seem unusual that people could so
easily share the gospel message at just the time when
others are open to witness? Do you find it hard to
believe that Christians could minister to people who
appear not to have time for anything, not even to
receive ministry? It is impossible for the church to
lead anyone on its own to this kind of genuine care
unless the church is led by the Holy Spirit.

Letting Him Make It Happen

Leadership is an important virtue for the church. In
Western cultures where winning and losing are
important values, the church is pressured to make the
right moves, be seen at the right times and have a
winning team in the eyes of the community. Making
decisive decisions, giving on a grand scale and making a mark are important attributes for a church in
contemporary society. These phrases are descriptive
of such modern virtues as progress, vision and success. But the difference between ministry and "success" is in leadership. The motivations of leadership
in the market, the media and the mall are not the

same as mentors for ministry. The church is led into further ministry by the Holy Spirit, not by individuals in the church. The leadership of the church begins by following the ministry of the Holy Spirit.

Leading by following the Holy Spirit is especially important in becoming a caring church. The Holy Spirit continually provides care for those in the church; thus the issue of care centers around the church's relationship with the Spirit. God's work, especially that of the Holy Spirit, is the origin of care. Without the leadership of the Spirit, care becomes humanistic. The church's claim to care is valid only so long as it follows the Spirit's leadership. The temptations of care leadership for the modern church are twofold.

1. *The first temptation is to think that the problems and needs of the hurting and needy are beyond the scope and ability of the Holy Spirit.* Hurting people isolate themselves and sometimes become suspicious. They may not allow you to approach them easily, even though they are desperately hurting inside. Nevertheless, the Holy Spirit is already working in the life of even the most difficult person. The believer's confidence is not in his or her own ability to break the crusty shell wrapped around a hurting heart; it is in following the leading of the Spirit.

The Holy Spirit is always working in people's hearts. It is not a question of "if" or "whether," the question is how or in what way the Spirit is working. Before we can conceive of how to care for another, the Spirit has already birthed the care of the Father's love in that person. The key, then, is to follow the work of the Spirit's care.

2. *The second temptation is to feel that the Holy Spirit can do the work of care and may never need the assistance of the believer.* To the contrary, the Spirit's work of care always incorporates the work of the believer. God has constructed the world, and His design is to include the believer as a necessary, constant part of the caring process. The Holy Spirit prepares a person's heart for a caring ministry before that person becomes aware of another's need.

The Spirit has someone in mind for us to care for before we are aware of who the person is and what the need is. After He prepares us for caring ministry, the Spirit brings us to the awareness of others who need our care. The Spirit then leads us to speak, act, pray and minister a host of other actions in the care of the needy person.

Godly Care Versus Good Intentions

Christian care is a Spirit-led process that constantly recruits and uses believers. When a believer resists the process, it diminishes the care that the needy receive. It is not that the Holy Spirit needs the believer to care, but rather that the person in need receives care in increased quality and quantity when believers follow the leading of the Spirit.

The care process can also be misdirected. The Christian reverts to a self-centered form of care when the Holy Spirit is not followed. A person may do many things to care for others, but this may not be what the person specifically needs if the Holy Spirit is not leading. A cause may be advanced, a plan enacted or a budget delivered; but care may not have taken place because the resources were directed by human sympathy rather than by divinely directed care.

Where Are You Going?

In John 13, the disciples faced a dilemma. Perhaps, this was their greatest dilemma since they started following the Master. They had just eaten the Last Supper with the Lord (v. 4), and experienced moments of blessing and confusion. Jesus had washed their feet in an act of servanthood (see vv. 4-20).They had seen Judas rush into the night (vv. 21-30), and now Jesus was telling them that He himself was going away (vv. 31-35).

Thoughts raced through their minds. They asked several questions (13:36—14:22). They sought to know where Jesus was going, asking to go with Him. Jesus told them that although He was going away, in a sense He would still be with them.They wondered aloud how Jesus could be gone, but still be with them. He endeavored to answer their questions with care and sensitivity. He knew that their continued service to Him, their love for each other and their ministry to the world was at stake.

The risks were high, because the essential issue of leadership was at stake. There was still much for the disciples to learn. They had to continue to be loving disciples, and they had to become an arm of compassion reaching into the world. The possibility that they would follow another was real. They may break into infighting, lacking the love He had sought to engender between them. And they may depart away from His agenda of transforming lives and seek their own paths for caring for the world.

Judas had already taken his own path, thinking he was changing the world for the better. Sincere and zealous, Judas wanted to release his people from the bondage of the oppressors. He thought Jesus was leading a movement that would release them from the grip of the government occupying Judah.

Jesus' agenda was different. It was not necessarily a difference in purpose—both sought to care for Judah by relieving the people of oppression and breaking the bonds of tragedy that permeated their hearts and homes. Jesus' message was centered around Himself as the Messiah, however. His own sacrifice and His disciples would become transforming instruments of mercy. Judas wanted to rebel against the evil empire and make the restoration of the religion of his forefathers the ruling state. Judas was tragically wrong. The other disciples, however, followed the leadership of the Lord instead.

In verse 26, Jesus reveals the key. He says that through the Holy Spirit He would be with them, leading and guiding their care for one another. They would continue to follow Him by following the Holy Spirit. The Holy Spirit would minister peace and care to them personally, in the same manner in which He had led them while He was on earth. They would experience the same care and leadership they received when

He was physically with them. They would do the same works of ministry — even greater ones — as they continued to follow Him by following the Holy Spirit.

The transition to the leadership of the Holy Spirit was crucial for the disciples. The future and genuineness of their ministry was at stake. Jesus wanted them and their ministry to be true and caring. This truth of character would be possible only as they followed the Holy Spirit. Jesus identified the Holy Spirit as the Spirit of truth repeatedly, as He explained to them how they were to follow the Spirit (see 15:26 — 16:33). The Holy Spirit's leadership and their faithfulness in following the Spirit were Christ's guarantee of genuine discipleship, ministry and care.

They were to be filled with the Spirit; the Holy Spirit would actually dwell within them. A major purpose of the infilling and Baptism in the Holy Spirit was so the Spirit could lead them. The indwelling Spirit would only have to whisper to their spirits, and they would follow His guidance. The Spirit within them would be the source of power for their long journey into a hurting world. This presence was also a source of joy as they encountered the pain and sorrow.

A Strategic Response for the Church

In addition to developing a guiding vision (ch. 2), listing its most critical values (ch. 3), moving toward transformation and becoming a caring church by equipping people to minister together (ch. 4), and determining who to reach (ch. 5), a church must be trained in the ministries of compassion, and especially in following the leadership of the Holy Spirit. Every church can potentially be mobilized as an army of care—well-trained, adequately equipped and focused on the hurting, hungry and needy of the church, community and world.

Every army needs training. A new recruit receives basic training in preparation for years of service. The fundamental skills of combat and readiness are repeatedly drilled into the soldier. The first and most constant lesson in the recruit's training is the line of authority. Without the correct protocol of command—who is in command, how to take orders and how to follow leadership during the heat of battle—the army is scattered and the cause is lost.

The army of care in a local church must also be effective leaders. Certainly the leadership role of the pastor, elders and ministry leaders, as well as policies and procedures, need to be communicated. The knowledge of the leadership of the Holy Spirit must be a priority in each soldier of care. Sensitivity training, responsiveness and guidance under the Holy Spirit must be taught. Believers learning to care need experience where they carefully observe and experience the advantages of following the leading of the Spirit. A church *can* decisively and accurately reach within and without, caring and making a difference in the lives of those around it.

They Are Still There

Jim, Sandy and Frank go to your church. They work with you and live in the homes of the towns around you. They continue to have needs, hurts and crises. How can a common strategy target them with the adequate help and care they need? How can anyone know the feelings that beat in their hearts, and the care that would find the rhythms of brokenness pulsating through their lives? Is there a way to monitor the momentum of their cries when no one is around? The only way is to follow the leadership and care of the Spirit.

The Holy Spirit is still with them. His care never stops. Whatever their location, condition or crisis, the Holy Spirit is next to the hurting spot in their hearts, delivering the right amount of God's love and care. Jim, Sandy and Frank may not recognize it, they may even reject it, but the Spirit's care never stops.

Hopefully, those within the body of Christ are still there as well. Hopefully, we'll still find the preacher and the congregation at each church service following the care of the Spirit in ministering to Jim. Betty will be able to continue to meet Sandy at lunch break and be sensitive to what the Holy Spirit may be doing in Sandy's life. And Harry will be able to work long enough by Frank's side until Frank comes to know the Lord.

The church, Betty and Harry must be there, because the care of the Spirit would be incomplete without their ministry.

STRATEGIC TRANSFORMATION STEP
Commit to a training program that teaches
people to be sensitive to the Spirit's care.

PROCEDURE TO DEVELOP
Make training a vital part of care,
especially the ministry leadership.

IMPLICATIONS FOR CARE
The work of care in the local body continues
in harmony with the care of the Spirit.

---7---

ACCOUNTABILITY AND THE ABUSE OF CARE

A church must be accountable enough to be a sensitive church. An absence of care is not just the absence of passion, it is the abuse of passion. The church may be passionate about many things, but if care does not temper the sentiment of the church, then passion becomes abrasive. Like love, without care the work of the church is nothing (see 1 Corinthians 13).

Care seeks to do the will of God by carefully applying the work of God to those in need. Good deeds without care are instruments of deception, because our actions say one thing and our hearts say another. The genuineness of care is important because God not only requires needs to be met, but He also desires that vessels of care accurately reflect Him.

Walking Away

Alone, Vickie walks down the aisle, through the

sanctuary doors, past the handshaking and out into the world, wondering about what just happened. *Why doesn't someone talk to me?* she wonders. *Did anyone notice I was here? If I hadn't come today, would it have made any difference? My Sunday school teacher said she was glad I came. The person who sat next to me had a nice smile, the pastor was friendly. I liked what I saw, but I wonder if everybody else knows everybody else. Where are they going now; are they going somewhere together? Did I miss something?* She continued to wonder to herself.

Vickie, like everyone else in the community around the church, received a letter that week from the Friendly Church: *The Church With a Heart.* The letter came at just the right time for Vickie. Living alone, never married, she had been trying to make it on her own, away from family and friends. She left home two years ago, full of hopes and dreams, ready to meet new people and find new opportunities. College occupied her time for the first year, but her money ran out. She has a good job, but the bills have been piling up. She hasn't really developed any relationships; for some reason, it has been hard for her to get to know people.

She received another letter, a thank-you note, for attending the church service. Reading the card, she remembered the church service. No one spoke to her except the greeter—not one conversation, not one question, no information volunteered. The letter and brochure last week were nice, and the letter this week was nice; but her experience *in* church did not match what the mail promised. She turned the original letter over and saw that it was sent to "Resident." Re-reading it, she saw that it was addressed to "Dear

Neighbor Friend." She remembered friends back home and wondered what it would be like to have and be a friend in a church.

The Smiths live outside of the mailing area of the church. They did not receive a letter or brochure last week, but they know about the church. They see the church van pass by on Saturdays and Sundays. They don't really know where the van is going or what it is doing in their neighborhood, but they are familiar with the church for another reason. They recognize the name of the church and the slogan *The Church With a Heart*. This is the church that comes on holidays and gives them a special box of groceries.

The groceries are nice and the person who delivers them is usually wearing a friendly smile, the but Smiths often wonder who the people are that deliver the food. They gave their names, but the Smiths never saw them again. The Smiths told them they were interested in church, but they never heard anything else. They responded to a questionnaire and noted their interest in Sunday school for the children, but no one ever came back. The Smiths appreciate the help from the "Heart Church," as they call it. They really would like to go to the church, but they don't know how to get in touch with them. The Smiths don't have a phone, and they don't recognize the address on the van as it zooms by.

Last Thanksgiving they noticed the writing on the sack delivered to them and thought it might have been a name—maybe their name. Looking closer, they saw that someone had written a code with the number 4 on the bag. They didn't know what the number meant; their apartment number is 5.

Are Vickie and the Smiths ungrateful for what the church with a heart has done for them? Absolutely not. Vickie was glad for the mail, the only mail from any church she had received since being in town. The Smiths' holiday was special because of the gift from the church. They were grateful because without the box of additional groceries, they would not have had much to eat. The box made their holiday special.

But what the mail and food did was to whet Vickie's and the Smiths' appetite for more. The invitation to friendship led Vickie to seek out a friend at the church. The theme of "heart and feeling" caused her to genuinely look for the warmth that would touch her heart when she visited the church. The thank-you letter made her want even more to receive what was promised.

Unfortunately, none of these things happened. She observed friendly people, but they were friendly with each other. She felt the warmth of a church with a heart, but no one even had a conversation with her. When she noticed on the letter and envelope that the church did not really know who she was, she was disappointed. She felt as though she received an invitation and showed up at the door but one let her in.

The Smiths would like to talk to the people who deliver food from the church. The kids have asked their parents a lot about going to Sunday school, but their parents have had to tell them they don't have a telephone, and they don't know the address of the church. No one has ever returned to their home to tell them more. The children are disappointed and feel neglected.

Merry Christmas

Do these stories sound like I am harsh on the church? At least the church did *something* to try to reach Vickie and the Smiths. The congregation did more than many other churches in the surrounding community. However, have you ever received a Christmas gift, thanked the one who gave the gift and discovered by the surprise on the face of the person that he or she did not know about the gift? Or the person had forgotten about purchasing the gift? Even worse, the person could not remember your name? That feeling in the pit of your stomach is what Vickie and the Smith children felt.

Gifts from the church to the community without corresponding follow-up, reduces the effects accomplished by commendable actions. This sets the recipients up for possible disappointment. In a world with massive problems of human need and agony, no entity holds more promise for society today. The church stands at the critical vortex of all of the pain felt by families falling apart, children growing up without care and individuals living without food and shelter. The expectations, images and promises believers communicate to the community are from Scripture and from the role society has given it. They are filled with promise.

The problem occurs when the church falls short of delivering what is promised. The promises themselves are not erroneous; the church is the single institution in society that holds divine promise and has the ability to offer the very presence of Christ himself. It is even more critical when the church uses what it promises to simply paint itself to be something it is not. Care becomes calloused, love becomes hypocritical and benevolence becomes abrasive.

Care Is Careful

The injunctions of Scripture calling the church to care for the world indicate a long process rather than an occasional activity. We must reach the life of a person, and not merely press for a decision. Christ commissioned His disciples to reach others, not merely join a campaign to invite others to a church service. The world is waiting to genuinely use some short-term responses from the church. However, what the church really needs and what Christ intended was for the church to follow up on its immediate impulse to care with long-term interest and personal engagement.

The church's mandate is to change lives, not just provide a supper. Give the supper, but sit down and visit after the meal. Go back to the person's house for the next meal . . . and the next. Get to know the parents, the children and as many of the family as you can. Take visitors more seriously. Talk to them. Learn their names, their interests and especially their needs. Do what Christ did: Dwell with the people (see John 1:2-7). Walk and talk with them as He did with the disciples. Go for a real life change, not just a good attendance on a special Sunday. Feed them the Bread of Life by getting to know them for several meals instead of just on a special holiday.

In Scripture, the mission of the church never outlines a short-term commitment; instead it calls for a life-changing dedication to reaching and affecting lives. The church is to actually visit often in the homes of the community. We are to treat those who want to be a part of the body of Christ as though they are. Christ followed up His invitation to new life by ministering to the whole person.

Scriptural Instruction

Paul was essentially involved with those he reached out to. He instructed them about life changes, not just about momentary decisions at an altar. When he exhorted the congregation at Ephesus, he demonstrated genuine, lasting concern for their lives. He instructed them about the love of Christ, but was also concerned that they love each other (4:25). He wanted them to experience the joy of Christ, but he also wanted them to live a life of emotional control (vv. 26, 27). He offered them the gift of life in Christ, but he emphasized that they were not to steal from each other (v. 28). He wanted them to receive the words of life, but he also wanted them to speak edifying words to each other (v. 29).

Paul became dynamically involved with the people to whom he ministered. He was concerned about them; he followed up, finding out whether they were really living for Christ. He wanted to know whether the church was really ministering to them and whether they were truly growing in Christ. Paul's love and care was followed up with the church's own continued love and ongoing care. That extra step made Paul a church builder as well as a church planter.

First Corinthians 12 offers further evidence of Paul's long-term commitment to following up on those he reached. He wanted them to feel each other's burdens, to exhibit the same care for one another, to feel the others' pain and celebrate their joys (12:25, 26). Care was a part of them; consequently, they were a part of each other. They were not satisfied with merely being a gifted church (vv. 8-11); that was incomplete. They were a church where believers cared for each other and the world extensively. To communicate everlasting love, they practiced long-lasting care.

The question "What does it take to care?" must be preceded by an examination of our commitment to care. Half-hearted or short-term care is like a child's unfulfilled promise. It becomes a friend's return that never happens. It becomes a handout from a withdrawn hand. Jesus came, stayed with us and even gave His life for us. Paul went to the ends of the earth, stayed and worked until real change occurred in lives. Can the church care without adequately following up on its caring actions? Does the person searching for a caring church have to run to catch up with a busy pastor or a distracted congregation? Will the net result of years of labor by a church simply be the repeating of short-term acts of care? Or will it be a life of care?

A Strategy for the Church

In addition to developing a guiding vision (ch. 2), listing its most critical values (ch. 3), moving toward transformation and becoming a caring church by equipping its people to minister together (ch. 4), determining who to reach (ch. 5), and training in the ministries of compassion (ch. 6), a church must also hold itself accountable for care. A plague of the modern church is "short-termitis."

The church around the corner may have started and forgotten more programs than it has choruses showing on its overhead projector. The world has no idea what the church does through the week. It may see one or two short-term acts in behalf of the community through the year; but what long-term, sustained ministry of care does the community see coming from the church on the corner? Many churches *do* have programs that have contributed for years to those who are in need. The tragedy, however, is that they are the exceptions rather than the rule.

In a closet somewhere in most churches are visitors cards. Often they are thrown away and forgotten. Unfortunately, many churches use them to welcome the visitors from the pulpit and to send follow-up letters or make calls — but that is all. Food may be distributed to houses, but nothing is known about the people who live in the house. Who are they? Do they have other needs? When can the church make the next visit to the home?

The strategy of the local church must include accountability for its acts of care. Names, addresses, profiles, visits and other methods of retrieving critical information is vital. This information is the bedrock of long-term care. The church must follow up on people who are still in the worship setting. Follow up on them when they get home and even in the marketplace throughout the week.

The classroom must become the launching pad for a sustained effort to follow up on the progress each student in Sunday school or other classes is making. Teachers must know where their students live, and what they do the other six-and-a-half days of the week. Superintendents must follow up with visits, not just count up totals on Sunday morning. Elders must lead the congregation in care, not just approve a budget. They must be guardians and prayer warriors over the spiritual life of the church.

A caring church doesn't just visit a neighborhood, it enters the community in the way Christ did, dwelling among the people, walking with them, knowing them and bearing their burdens. A caring church does not just seek a higher attendance average, but yearns for a higher level of spiritual maturity. A caring church holding itself accountable is more interested in the completion and follow-through of a program than the start-up and excitement at the beginning. The needy have seen the start-ups and short-term acts of care; the community is waiting for the staying and the long-term presence of a church that truly cares.

Knowing Who You Care About

What would happen if Vickie received an invitation Sunday morning as she was leaving her seat to come immediately to a special reception hosted by the pastor and his wife? What if she walked in and people knew her name, because they had become acquainted with the visitors cards? What if the pastor and his wife took time to know her, and learned of her leaving home and her lonely time in the community? What if others took the time to talk to her, to find out how she's doing and whether she has any special needs? Then that night someone would call her and invite her to come to a social activity the singles in the church were sponsoring. There are only two or three singles, but they would like for Vickie to join them. What if the Sunday school class she attended continued to encourage her, taking turns calling and visiting with her?

A year later, Vickie not only would have people in the church she knew, but she would be like them—caring, reaching and changing other lives for Christ.

What would happen if the church stopped by the Smiths every Saturday, bringing food they needed? The church would come to know the Smiths and would find that they have a legitimate need for assistance. Mr. Smith has a full-time job, but it is not enough for the family's needs. Mrs. Smith works part-time while the children are in school, but there is still not enough money for food, rent, bills, clothes and other needs.

What if Sunday school workers who work with children stopped by to visit with the Smith children, making sure they become a part of the church's children's ministry. What if the church helped the Smiths get a telephone? After a few months, someone in the church who knows a business owner might be able to help Mr. Smith get a better job.

A year later the Smiths would be just like the people in the church. They would be one of them on Saturdays, reaching out to other families in their community.

They would be transformed and becoming like Christ, who lived and walked among the people He reached out to, laboring with them until their lives were changed.

STRATEGIC TRANSFORMATION STEP
Develop a method of follow-up and accountability to ensure that genuine care is realized.

PROCEDURE TO DEVELOP
Implement a long-term method of reporting and follow-up.

IMPLICATIONS FOR CARE
Viable, long-term programs and transformation replaces a parade of short-term programs.

8

GOOD INTENTIONS ARE NOT ENOUGH

A church must be aware of the necessity for single-mindedness. A church can desire to fulfill its God-given mission, and its actual work not match the desire. Programs may not match principles. Reflecting its heart and pursuing an agenda that denies what it is saying, the church may verbalize its intentions, while communicating by its actions that its actual priorities do not include care.

If the language of intentions is not the same as the language of priorities, a church will be known by those within and without the church as inconsistent. A lack of care is compounded by inconsistent communications. The church that is double-minded about care is hypocritical and lacks a basic, underlying authenticity of ministry.

Bring Your All to the Altar

Phil felt the dampness in the palm of his hands.

He looked down and saw a puddle of tears on the altar. He felt so clean. His heart had been aching to go to the altar, and he was glad he did. Although people were around him that morning, all Phil could do was focus on what the pastor was saying. His heart was racing, but he was at peace. He felt not an ounce of worry. He wished he could stay at the altar, because he wanted to feel this way all the time.

Just then an arm came to rest on his shoulders. He didn't know who was kneeling next to him, but the man had a warm smile. The man asked, "How do you feel, brother?" Phil nodded in the affirmative, because he could not speak just yet. He could barely swallow. He was nervous, happy and cautious all at the same time.

"Do you feel like you have made things right with the Lord?" asked the gentleman. Phil nodded again. Actually, he had been a Christian, even a church leader for a long time. He remembered he was with strangers that day; he had just come by to visit. "Please write down your name and address. We want to get in touch with you and let you know you are loved here. We want to reach out to you. We're so glad you came to the altar," the gentleman spoke, emphasizing every word.

Phil was overcome. People really cared! Finally, someone cares! Phil could feel himself relax, not with the Lord but with the gentleman. Taking the pen and card, he filled out his name and address. *This is going to be wonderful. Finally, there is someone I can talk to about all this stuff my family and I have been going through,* he thought to himself.

Phil's family was not there that morning. It was hard for his wife, Julie, and their three children, Mike, 6, Joey, 9, and Jill, 10, to come to church. Julie lived somewhere between angry and depressed (usually the latter), and the kids were confused. All kinds of things were happening in Phil's life, and he did not understand most of them.

He was a professional who had been fired from his job after 18 years. He had messed up big time, disappointing his wife and nearly losing his marriage and family. People looked at him differently. Before, he would walk through town and everyone would greet him with respect; now he had to bypass people because it was too painful — for them as well as for himself.

Phil knew it would be bad if his secret sin was revealed, but he had no idea he would go through the grueling wilderness of alienation he had experienced. He could not fathom what his family must be going through. His wife withdrew, crawling into a cave of depression. The 6-year-old was playful, but he was still full of questions about why he had to leave his friends at church. He still called them on the telephone, but he couldn't understand why they didn't come over to his house as before. The middle child started having trouble in school. His daughter crawled into her own cave, crying a lot at night. Even worse, she would pull away when he tried to hold her.

It had been two and a half months since he heard the chilling words that ended 18 years of following his beloved vocation. He was suspended for a year from doing what he knew best, and given another year on probation before he would be allowed to do what he felt God had called him to do. He knew his sin was not right, but the impact of the problem was greater than he ever imagined.

At the altar that morning, the burden of guilt lifted as Phil made things right with God. The gentleman praying with him said he would be getting in touch. Things were beginning to change. The pastor had preached about making and receiving a commitment from God. "If we will take the first step, He will take two," the pastor said. "And we'll be right there with you, helping you every step of the way."

Two weeks later Phil was a changed man. No, he was not on the road to recovery, he was back in the same rut, following the same path that destroyed his working life and his family's world. For the first couple of days after praying at the altar, he did pretty well. On Wednesday he began to struggle. How he wished he had the name of the man who placed his arm around him and took his name and telephone number. By Friday, after no contact at all, it began to sink in—no one from the church was going to call.

This was a rough week. His wife told him she could not live in the same town anymore. The looks from people and the alienation were too much for her. The daughter and oldest son were fighting all the time. The youngest son was starting to have nightmares.

Meanwhile, as Phil drove around town, thinking about giving in to the temptation that took his vocation and credentials away, he suddenly realized that for the first time in his life, he didn't know what the

family was going to do. He was three months behind
on the house payments, and he had no money coming in.

Care—Intention or Priority?

The pastor happened to notice Phil's card on the
altar Sunday morning on his way to the back of the
church to shake hands with everyone as they left.
What he didn't know was that Harold, the altar
worker who spoke to Phil on Sunday, had left the
card for Alice to pick up.

Alice and Harold attended the same training
class two years ago for altar workers. During this
excellent time of training, the pastor and altar workers decided to collect the prayer and convert cards
by having the altar workers leave them on the altar
for Alice to pick up. Six months later, Alice missed
a couple of Sundays because her grandchildren
were sick and she had to help take care of them.
During this time Bob, the head usher, started pick-
ing the cards up when he was cleaning. He placed
them in the storage room.

When Alice came back to church, she began working in the nursery, because she felt her grandchildren
needed extra care. Therefore, she didn't resume pick-
ing up the prayer cards, but Bob continued to do it.

In the meantime, the pastor thought the altar
workers were taking care of the follow-up.

Does this scenario sound unusually complicated?
So are the reasons for the lack of follow-up in ministries of care. They range from not having enough
time and thinking that someone else is doing it, to
believing that if people are really sincere or really

want to change their lives, they will simply keep coming back to church. What may be missed here is that Phil's life has gone from a week-to-week cadence to a moment-by-moment countdown. He's three months behind on his rent, has no savings and his family is falling apart.

The problem is that Phil brought all his problems to the altar and walked away with the church's promises to minister to him. The church has good intentions, and so does Phil. He was promised that he would be contacted, but he waited in vain. The church waited, but not to care for Phil. They waited for other things that pressed them, things that crowded out the church's ability to care for him. All the things the church did was good; they were the priorities of the church. Sadly, care and follow-up were intentions, but not priorities.

The church often sees the needs of the fallen and hurting like Phil and salves its concern with a stroke of intention. The intentions are sincere and emotional, they give temporary relief. Feeling good, the church is able to move on to its priorities. Even Phil had a temporary good feeling because of the work at the altar and the church's intention. The tragedy is that intentions are inadequate and deceptive. The intention to care leaves the church deceiving itself and those to whom it has promised care—unless care becomes a priority.

No Room for Intentions

Intentions to care are only understood by those who have the intentions. To the thirsty, tired and hungry of the world, intentions are a luxury long forgotten. Intentions without follow-up become tools of deception. The intention to help perpetuates an excuse not to help. Eventually the person and the church begin to confuse intentions with action. The feeling evolves that if we intended to help, it will be understood by the needy and the poor. After all, God knows our hearts are in the right place. Then the desire to do good is perceived to be adequate, and in some cases superior, to showing we care. But the waiting world cannot see our intentions, because our priorities get in the way.

What were the motives and intentions of the Savior? When He was moved with compassion, what translated that feeling into care? Would He have stopped by the wayside for any other reason? Did other priorities consume the Savior's time? These questions are worth asking, because some priorities can become distractions. Would the New Testament writings reveal Jesus struggling with competing passions or puzzling about priorities? Is there an example where He wanted to care, but was not able to get around to it? When He began to care was He distracted or just not able to care? Was the fact that He intended to enough?

Such a search would reveal that Christ never did any of these things. He demonstrated the truth that intentions are never enough. If Jesus had only left behind Him the best of intentions, the gospel would have stopped. His mission would have been incomplete, and Christ would not have died on the cross. He did not teach good intentions as something to follow. In reality, good intentions are the vice of the church.

Don't Get Caught "In the Meantime"

The poor, the needy, the lonely and the neglected wait on the sidelines of the church. If we will turn away from ourselves and look at those on the sidelines, we'll see the arms of the Master around them. While the Savior holds the hurting, the church sits on the fringe of His mercy. The story in John 4:1-42 illustrates how followers of the Lord were standing on the sidelines. The disciples were busily filled with priorities, but woefully empty of care.

Jesus and the disciples reached the town of Sychar, and the need for ministry was so great that Jesus had to stay two days. The town was not large, but it was well known. Located at a major crossroads, Jacob's well was a significant resting place there. The village's reputation was the "drunken town," an ancient derivative of its name *Sychar*.

John told us about the woman at the well, but the disciples may have been as much, if not more, of His focus. They were busy in ministry, baptizing those who came to Jesus (v. 2). When the woman approached the well (v. 7), the disciples went to town to buy lunch (v. 8). Jesus noticed the woman at the well and perceived her need for ministry. So He proceeded to minister to her, sharing the news of the living water available through Him.

This woman in desperate need presented several layers of religious, cultural and social resistance. Jesus ministered the care and compassion of the heavenly Father to her, promising her living water to satisfy her thirsting heart. She wore a shell of resistance in order to hide a life of pain. She visited the well at the hottest part of the day, when no one else was

GOOD INTENTIONS ARE NOT ENOUGH

there. Her reputation for immorality had alienated
her from the people in the small town. Jesus saw
her life of confusion, pain and hunger for God,
however. He confronted her about five previous
husbands and her current live-in companion.

Christ's ministry was more than intentions. Good
intentions would have given up earlier and gone to
town. Intentions alone probably would not have
noticed her, because other priorities superceded
her. People with good intentions might have seen
the woman coming and left when she offered the
first signs of resistance. The woman responded to
Christ's promise of living water. In verses 25 and
26, Christ presented Himself as the Messiah and the
woman came to accept Him as the Messiah.

Instead of telling us the woman's reaction when
she accepted Christ, however, John chose to describe
the disciples' reaction. At the moment the woman's
life was changed, the disciples arrived back at the
well (v. 27). While she was calling on the Messiah,
the disciples were coughing up criticism. They did-
n't ask the woman if she needed help, nor did they
ask Jesus if He needed assistance in ministering to
her. They were concerned about eating. The priority of taking care of themselves crowded out any
intent to care.

When the woman left her water pot to go into the
town and tell others in need about Jesus, the narra-
tive shows us the contrast. The woman was rescuing others and the disciples were caught "in the
meantime" (v. 31). Jesus told them He had been ful-
filling a greater priority, but they still missed the
point. When the scores of villagers ran up the hill to

the well, Jesus urged the disciples to look at them. He described the approaching crowd as the harvest: "Do you not say, 'There are still four months and then comes the harvest'? Behold, I say to you, lift up your eyes and look at the fields, for they are already white for harvest!" (v. 35).

They missed it that day. No matter how much they had intended to do good, they walked right by a whole town in need. They had been blinded by the fact that other things had become more important to them. Their priority that day was to get lunch so they could do more baptizing. Their intentions were good, but they needed more than good intentions. Consequently, they walked past the woman and a whole town in need of care, while they were on the way to satisfy other priorities.

Strategic Response and Strategy of the Church

In addition to developing a guiding vision (ch. 2), listing its most critical values (ch. 3), moving toward transformation and becoming a caring church by equipping its people to minister (ch. 4), determining whom it will reach (ch. 5), training itself in the ministries of compassion (ch. 6), and holding itself accountable for care (ch. 7), a church must develop policies and procedures that match its intentions to minister to the poor, the needy and the hurting. This requires a review of each ministry and how it cares for others. The church must ask, "Do we actually get the job done? Are there forgotten steps, miscommunications and other priorities getting in the way of actually caring for people?"

An analysis of what is actually being done and what is not being done will enable you to match actual ministry with promises of care. Develop and review procedures to make sure that persons in need in the community received the assistance they may have been promised. Be sure that persons who pray at the altar receive a call and follow-up from the church, and that those who have been promised a friendly hand of fellowship are not left standing outside looking at the cliques and groups within the church.

Following Up On Intentions

Just as the evil spirit went back to the empty house in Matthew 12:45, the demon returned to Phil, but the church did not. Could the church have done things differently? Let's dream again. What if the church Phil attended that Sunday had not let him walk out the door alone? What if someone had sat down and talked with him in a follow-up conversation and, perhaps, discovered his tragic fall and the difficult time his family was having.

What if, after praying with Phil again, the caring Christian had taken the next step and transcribed Phil's information on two other cards for special assignments by the altar worker doing the follow-up after the service. What if someone was assigned to call Phil and visit him that week? What if after inviting him to next Sunday's service, he had met him and sat with him during the service? What if, in the meantime, the altar worker had placed one of the cards in a box outside the pastor's office?

Does this sound like a lot of work? Genuine Christian care has to be more than good intentions. There are too many "Phils" left waiting in our communities.

Sometimes we don't understand the problem. It is not that the people do not visit our churches. It is not that the churches do not have good services. They minister to people like Phil at the altar. The problem is that we have left Phil on the altar of good intentions, failing to follow through with our ability to care. Good intentions cannot replace the step-by-step process of maintaining care as the priority of the church.

STRATEGIC TRANSFORMATION STEP
Develop step-by-step procedures to assure that care is actually accomplished.

PROCEDURE TO DEVELOP
Analyze how each ministry accomplishes the goals of care.

IMPLICATIONS FOR CARE
The priorities of the body are matched with the intentions of the church to care.

9

STEPPING THROUGH THE DOORWAY AND STAYING OUTSIDE

A church must be aware enough to be an extended church. By its very nature the gospel is constantly reaching beyond boundaries of comfort and familiarity to those outside its circumference. Once a person becomes a believer, that person is mandated to reach out to others. Unfortunately, the modern church has made preaching equivalent to reaching—the preacher may reach someone, but not the church. Genuine care will change this and reach those beyond us. It will expand our vision and take us to people we not only do not know, but also someone we may have never considered knowing.

Stepping Out to Others

What kind of people come to the church on the corner? What kind of people do believers want to come to their church? What kind of people do they not want to come to their church? What kind of people would cause believers to stop coming to church if those other kind of people attended? Who are these people? Would the church on the corner have a particular person in mind, or are these just general categories or images in their hearts?

Joey changed his name. Cush, the name he has taken, stands for someone who is able to slide in and out of alternative realities. The name came to him while he was playing a group game on the Internet. He plays every third night and has built quite a following. A lot of people want to be part of his group. He has developed a lot of codes and secret passageways. He has a lot of power built up, but its not the kind of mystic power you have to have to be a "master" at other levels.

Cush/Joey spends just about all of his waking time on the computer. He's 17 years old and ready to graduate from high school. He would like to travel to Europe and meet some of the masters he has met on the Net in the game he plays. Another ambition is to capture the next upgrade in computers he has read about on the Web.

Myra works hard at being accepted. She is in her 20s and trying to make a living, but she has encountered the artificial walls that exist between men and women. A line of missed opportunities, and embarrassing moments in front of colleagues at work have made her sensitive about the opinions males have of females. She knows some women could improve their attitudes toward men, but that does not make things easier for her.

Mary looks at the church and sees it as a male-dominated institution. Although she is not a feminist, she has been hurt at work by incidents between her and men. When she thinks about going to church, she thinks, *Will it be same, if not more, of what I have experienced at other places?*

Charles has been cautious about church for a long time. His grandmother, someone he really respected, was a praying woman. She raised Charles and his four brothers and sisters. His mom lived in the house, but she was busy working two jobs. She loved the kids, but she was never around. Being a minority, you would think he would be accustomed to being outnumbered. But he cannot get past the feeling that the church is a threat. The Lord is not the threat—it's the people in the church. Church people say a lot of things that isolate a lot of people.

Charles puts up with the double standard in the world, but why should he have to deal with it in church? It's just not worth it to him.

Carl goes *to* the church, but he has never been *in* the church on the corner. Every night, when he makes his rounds looking for whatever he can find, Carl stops behind the church, hoping no one will see him. He doesn't have a car, and that's good because no one can see him. Sometimes Carl leans against the wall, at other times he sits on the steps where, every night, he says a prayer. "The Lord honors faithfulness," Carl's preacher-dad always told him. So Carl comes to have church every night. Some nights he just sits. Other nights he cries, but every night he's faithful.

Chris and Irene Gonzalez have three children: Carlos, 6; Manuel, 11; and Enrique, 14. Manuel has a lot of problems at school. He has been diagnosed with Attention Deficit Hyperactivity Disorder (ADHD). The school officials have worked with the doctors to prescribe the proper medication. It has helped some; but at times, it just seems to get worse. Manuel doesn't sit still in class. He has motor tics that cause him to jerk. Around other kids, he can be a behavioral problem, talking loudly and often becoming belligerent.

Adults do not seem to understand. Their body language says to Chris and Irene, "What's wrong with your child? Can't he behave? Why don't you do something about that child? If you would just discipline him, he wouldn't act that way. Our kids don't act like that."

The thought of going to church is a problem for Chris and Irene. They've tried it a few times. Manuel was not allowed in class, because he was too much of a problem. Other parents treated him the same, maybe worse, than the people who do not go to church. Chris and Irene met in church. In fact, before they were married, they were both active in church. Now their children are growing up not knowing about church. They've tried, but it's just easier to stay at home.

The Color of Our Choices, the Comfort of Our Relationships

Everyone who drives by your church, my church and the church on the corner has made a decision. Each person has decided whether he or she is on the outside or on the inside of that church. Before they visit they have already made a decision about church in general and our church in particular. When they visit they are thinking, *Maybe I can be on the inside of this church and not on the outside.*

Church people tell you their church is open to everyone. The people who are not coming to church, however, have decided that for different reasons they cannot be a part of that church. What influences people to think they are not a part of a church? It may be culture, ethnicity, nationality, religion, past experience with churches, hurt within the family, a family that already goes to church and a host of other reasons.

Some think those outside the church just need to hear the gospel or receive an invitation to come. This is true in many cases. In other cases—perhaps in the majority of them—people have reasons for not coming to church. The real hurdle is finding a way to help nonattenders realize that there are no outsiders in the church on the corner.

No outsiders? What does it mean to have a church where there were no divisions among people? No barriers? No "walls" creating an outside and an inside? What would convince nonchurchgoers that they really are welcome? What element unites all people?

Perhaps the most common connecting link between all of us is care. This is the means God has given the church to transcend the barriers that divide us—especially those that divide the churchgoer from the person who finds it easy to stay at home.

In a caring church, a person can also connect with

the other most prominent common element among us—hurt. Caring is universal because hurting is universal. The search for a caring church persists because hurting persists. The church becomes caring when it realizes the searchers are the ones who hurt. They are not on their best behavior; they do not come with their best appearance. In fact, they can be disconcerting.

The society of the church is saturated by ideas of giftedness, success, health, wealth, liberty, unity and people who share the same values—or people just like us, creating a "body" of believers. Although these virtues are good and are promised in Scripture, they also delineate the culture of the nonchurchgoer. Those who do not attend church live contrary to these virtues and therefore see themselves as outsiders because they are so unlike us.

The challenge facing the church is to bridge the distance between the church and the world in these areas without compromising the church's identity. The experience of pain and the commonality of tragedy and grief caused by divisions of culture, race, ethnicity, poverty, hunger and many other conditions, are not threats to the identity of the church. Instead, they enhance it. The church's identity must be characterized by its affinity with the hurting. Its brand should be its empathy with the lonely. Its reputation should be its long, persistent effort to include others of diverse cultural and ethnic backgrounds.

Perhaps, the greatest challenge confronting the

care of the church in this century is multiculturalism. Our task is not merely to remove prejudice, it is to confront the issues concerning the expansion of who we are. The church is more than a single localized culture, it is one body composed of many cultures. We are not moving toward this new culture of Christ, we are already there.

Theological Assumptions

Love motivates the Christian to reach out to other believers *and* to the world. God sent His Son to die because of His love for the world. All who confess their sins, believe and serve Christ as Savior enter into the joys of Christ's love. This relationship between the Christian and the Lord is defined by love and ministry. Yet, an even deeper motivation forms the foundation of the love of the believer.

The foundation of the believer's love is care. This is Paul's message in 1 Corinthians 12 and 13. Chapter 13 is known as the Love Chapter. This love is important to the operation of the gifts of the Spirit within the body of believers. Between his exposition of the body of Christ, the church, and his explanation of the importance of love within the body, Paul establishes the importance of care. Laying a foundation for what he would say in chapter 13, Paul reminds believers that there should be no schism or split between them. They are to have "the same care for one another" (12:25). The message was clear: the power that bound them together was care, and the absence of care created the divisions between them.

The search for a caring church focuses attention on the necessary role of care in binding the church with those who are unlike it. The first step is to care for one another in the church and not allow a gulf to come between members of the body. The second step is to care for those in the world and not allow a rift to form between the church and the world. The church identifies with Christ himself, who identified with people in the world. He did not compromise His relationship with the heavenly Father, and neither should the church. But the church can and must enter into the world of the nonchurchgoer without compromising righteousness in Christ. The stronger a Christian's faith is in Christ and the deeper a church's commitment is to the Savior, the more they should be able to step outside of the four walls of the sanctuary into the world.

Caring When Misunderstood

The Samaritan, whose story is recorded in John 4, was unlike Christ and the disciples. First, she was a woman. To minister to her was to step outside of the bounds of some of the strict religious sects of the day. Next, she was a worldly person. To minister to a worldly person was to risk being misinterpreted by critical onlookers. Further, the woman did not believe the way Christ and the disciples believed.

Personal obstacles such as exhaustion and hunger could have distracted Jesus from witnessing to her. It would have been easy for Him to have said, "She is not like us; she is too critical. I don't have time to put up with this person who is so unlike Me." Instead of going with the disciples to town . . . or retreating inside the walls of Judaism . . . or hiding behind the curtain of pity because of personal criticism, Jesus remained outside of town with the woman until her heart was finally reached.

Caring for those who are different means a church will have to step outside its previous boundaries and reach those who don't look like them, act like them or share the same values.

Reaching Those Unlike Us

In addition to developing a guiding vision (ch. 2), listing its most critical values (ch. 3), equipping its people to minister together (ch. 4), determining who we will reach (ch. 5), training believers in the ministries of compassion (ch. 6), holding ourselves accountable for care (ch. 7), and developing policies and procedures that match our intentions to minister to the poor, the needy and the hurting (ch. 8), the church must also intentionally include those who are different, "not like us."

Care does not happen by default — it must be intentional. Those in need will not seek care before we seek them. This includes the task of extending who we are so we can persuade those who were once unlike us to become a part of us.

How many subcultures is our church comfortable with? A significant part, if not the heart, of the groups a caring church targets for ministry must include people unlike us. They may be young, like Joey/Cush, and cautious or insensitive to the world and priorities of older people. They may be female, like Myra, or male and cautious about gender issues, including feminism. They may be of another nationality, ethnicity or culture, and like Charles, cautious of racial reactions. They may be like Carl—poor, without a job, drifting socially.

They may even be suffering from a physical condition such as ADHD, like Manuel, exhibiting a behavior we do not understand. Going to each of these people, standing with them and not leaving them until they receive ministry is the difference between being a disciple merely on the way to lunch (John 4), or being a part of Jesus' ministry of caring.

A Pastor Steps Through a Doorway Labeled *Care*

The pastor of the church on the corner did not know what people would think, or even what his family might think. He proposed a new class for ADHD children. The Lord had been dealing with him about Manuel. He had met Chris and Irene at the mall, and noticed that they were having difficulty taking care of Manuel. Manuel wanted to go to another store and was shouting at his parents. The pastor felt like asking them if they needed some help, but thought they might tell him to get lost, or that it was none of his business.

When Chris and Irene looked up, however, something happened. Manuel looked at the pastor differently—as though he had something to give them. They visited in the mall, and other follow-up visits ensued for weeks. The pastor learned about ADHD and the nightmare Irene and Chris were experiencing.

The pastor also stopped by the church late one night and met Carl. His first inclination was to call the police because a stranger was hanging around the church was dangerous. Staying in his car, he asked Carl to come around to the front where there was more light. As they spoke briefly, the pastor invited him to come by in the morning. Something inside told Carl the pastor had something to offer him. They met the next morning, and the pastor invited Carl to come inside the church. The scene was moving. Carl had not been in a church sanctuary in 25 years. In the weeks that followed, the pastor heard Carl's story. He is still working with the homeless gentleman, giving him food and clothing from the church.

In various ways the pastor also came in contact with Charles, Myra and Joey/Cush. Each time, he felt the inward call to minister care in a tangible way. He didn't know exactly how the communication with each would go, but he knew he could not leave the place of ministry he had found with each of them. All three of these needy people felt the same thing. Gradually, they became convinced that this pastor and his church had something to offer them. They were thirsty and had been offered a drink of water.

The pastor knew criticism would follow. He was already getting comments from people in the congregation who felt he was neglecting them and bringing in people who are "not like us." The pastor knew, however, that he had stepped across a line—a line that was actually a doorway.

Having crossed that threshold and experienced the transformation taking place in the lives of the new people, he knew he could never go back to only ministering to those with whom he was comfortable.

STRATEGIC TRANSFORMATION STEP
Identify as a target for ministry those we consider different from us.

PROCEDURE TO DEVELOP
Plan for people who are unlike each other to minister together.

IMPLICATIONS FOR CARE
We become sensitive to ministry needs that we might otherwise miss.

———————10———————

WHEN WE HAVE CARED ENOUGH

A church must be aware enough to expand its limits. Instead of measuring our care by self-centered standards, the church must perceive the breadth of God's care. If God's work encompasses the world, then the church's care should be known by its expanding breadth, not its rigid limitations. Christian care is a constant, expanding process of including what and who we may have never thought of before.

Identifying the extent and expansion of our care is the task of every Christian. As an institution, the church is limited; as a body of believers, the church is constantly expanding. A caring church is not an institutional identity, tightly defined and preserved; it is an expanding, corporate entity that always reaches further and includes more people.

Enough is a Strange Word to Those in Need

Sharee could not believe it. Her husband, Ben,

had blown it again. This was the fifth job he had started and been fired from in a year. Every time they seemed to get a little ahead, Ben would blow it. Sharee cleaned an office building every night. Their children were tired of moving. There seemed to be no end in sight.

Roberta is 10 years old, but she has the physical body of an 8 year old because of malnutrition. She lives in the heart of one of the largest cities in the world, which is the major commercial center for the country. But Roberta is known to no one. She left her mother six months ago, because her mother was forcing her into prostitution. Her mother would beat her, then wait for a passerby to have pity on her. She taught Roberta to seduce the passerby and prostitute her body. Today, Roberta stands on the street, hoping for something to eat. There seems to be no end in sight.

Jim and Johnny are members of the church on the corner. They used to work closely in the church. They did a lot of good for a lot of people, donating time and resources to help the poor and disadvantaged. Then a slow process began that went from bad to worse. First, Jim became discouraged about a family he was trying to help that seemed to get no better. The more the church tried to help this family, the worse they became. The father couldn't hold a job, so they kept moving around the city.

Next, Johnny became discouraged for some reason about missions. It seemed to him that no matter how much the church helped a country, the more

they needed help. Feeding the poor, sending clothing and supporting street children did not seem to
make a difference. Johnny began complaining to
Jim, and Jim was complaining to Johnny.

Next, Jim and Johnny became irritated about
things in the church. Their general anxiety about not
making a difference in caring for the needy grew
until it affected their attitude toward the church.
They began to find fault with the teacher, the
preacher, the pews—even the length of the service.
Their irritability grew until it became personal.
They were personally offended by what they
believed to be neglect. They felt that no one in the
church cared for them when they were the ones
who needed care. Johnny said, "We need attention
just as much as those poor people we're always trying to help. What difference does it make anyway?"

They had made the transition from feeling that
they had to care for others to feeling that others
should care for them.

Wanting to Make a Difference

People in care ministries need to feel they are making a difference. It is tiring work serving the Lord by
serving others. Motivation focuses on changing lives.
The hope is that the poor will be lifted out of poverty,
drug addicts will recover, broken families will be
mended, the sick will be made well, the hungry will
be fed and those needing clothing will be clothed. At
times the list of needs seems endless. Sadly, many
care ministries in local churches come down to three,

two or just one person doing much of the work. Others in the church may not have the time, or simply may not have care in mind. Other churches do not have anyone doing care ministries.

One of the major tragedies in the ministry of caring is dealing with discouragement among the caregivers. Having to do much of the work — at times unnoticed — care workers become tired. But physical exhaustion is not nearly as serious as the mental, relational and eventually spiritual exhaustion that takes place. The wear and tear becomes especially acute when those needing care keep coming back. Little seems to be accomplished in some lives. Instead, things may appear to get worse.

The reality is that many lives *are* changed — dramatically. Millions are clothed and fed, and millions find shelter through ministries of care. Many workers in churches become discouraged, however, because they are intent on making a difference.

But care cannot be measured by the difference made in people's lives. Changing and transforming lives is important; yet, whether a church has successfully cared or not is measured by its persistence, not by its results. Care cannot be calculated in a boardroom. It cannot be judged by the pound. It cannot be held under the scrutiny of an inspector. The measure of a caring church goes beyond the lives that are helped.

A Persistent Virtue

A church's characteristic care must focus on the virtue of persistence that continues regardless of the response of the person being cared for. Care is not driven by the end product but by the compassion of God. God cares out of the abundance of His mercy and compassion. We are serving the caring God when we care for others. Service to God rather than service to humanity is the fuel that motivates us to reach the homeless. Devotion to the Master Caregiver is the driving force behind every food drive. Honoring the Father of mercies is the desire of those who bring hope to the homeless.

The caring church looks to God first, then to a desperate humanity. When the church focuses on Him, it can look intently and tirelessly at the needy. A persistent look to the caring Savior will keep the church refreshed to go continuously to a hopeless humanity. Marching to orders from the Lord, the church is able to make a difference in communities that are stricken by poverty.

Measure the success of your ministry by how well the church has heard, responded to and carried out the Lord's commission to care. Christian care is not a business but a mission. To the body of Christ, care is not a grant but a gift. Care in the community of faith is not a donation but a devotion. We care for others because God cared for us. The church gives of itself because God freely gave the gift of His Son. The church must continually go, despite the reception it receives, to the place of need.

How Much Is Enough?

"How long?" was the question Peter asked Jesus when Christ challenged him and the other disciples to care for one another by exercising forgiveness.

The challenge began with troubled relationships (see Matthew 18:1-14). Jesus challenged the disciples to go to someone who had offended them and personally seek reconciliation. If that wasn't successful, the disciples were to take another person with them. If still unsuccessful, they were to take still others. Ultimately, they were to recruit the entire church in order to reach the person in a spirit of care, forgiveness and reconciliation (Matthew 18:15-17).

Seeing the process as too involved, Peter grew weary thinking of the challenge. At this point Peter only wanted to care about the other person so long as the other person responded positively to his ministry. *What if the person does not respond? How long do I have to keep reaching out to that person?* So his question, "Lord, how often shall my brother sin against me, and I forgive him? Up to seven times?" (Matthew 18:21), was focused on response, not forgiveness.

Jesus replied by invoking the 70 x 7 rule. This is the standard of measurement for a caring church. No matter how little the person coming to Peter might have changed, Peter was to care and forgive. He was to forgive because of Christ's command, not because of what he saw take place in the life of the person. In the same way, the 70 x 7 rule applies to a caring church.

The Lord then told the disciples about the "accounts" (v. 23). An *account* referred to a standard of measurement and also to accountability. It meant we are responsible to the Lord for the way in which we care for others. Jesus said a servant, forgiven by a caring master, refused to forgive another who needed his care with the same spirit that was shown to him. The servant did not have "compassion" (vv. 27, 33). The servant was to care because his master had compassion on him. In the same way, the church is to care for others 70 x 7 times, because the Master has had compassion on us.

This story also illustrates the need of the church to be caring toward those in the church as well as those who are not saved. Although it is easy to become weary of caring when people in the church show little progress, we have to continue this vital ministry, whether the person in need of care is inside or outside the church.

The cost of not serving the Master of care is high. The servant who refused to show compassion 70 x 7 times was punished (vv. 34, 35). While the church weighs its successes of caring on the scales of improvement; it is, in truth, being held in the balance of the scales of God's compassion. God holds the church accountable to never stop caring, regardless of the response of those in need.

Measuring 70 x 7

In addition to developing a guiding vision (ch. 2), listing its most critical values (ch. 3), equipping its people to minister together (ch. 4), determining who it will reach (ch. 5), training in the ministries of compassion (ch. 6), holding itself accountable for care (ch. 7), developing policies and procedures that match its intentions to minister to the poor, the needy and the hurting (ch. 8), and including those who we think are "not like us" (ch. 9), the church must measure the success of its care by the 70 x 7 rule of Matthew 18.

Commitment to care, regardless of the outcome, is the heart of a caring church. Like a servant who has received the compassion of a loving master, the church willingly goes again and again to those in need. Like a servant consumed by compassion granted, those within a church are compassionate to minister to those inside the church. Like a servant given a second chance, the church gives the world another chance in the spirit of 70 x 7.

The stronger the unity of the church, the more it can reach the broken. The 70 x 7 rule means that the commitment to care continues until the Lord comes. The poor, hurting and the impoverished will always be in need of the church.

A caring church has a mandate to continue to care as long as someone is in need. A church council cannot ask if a care ministry is profitable for the church. A board of elders cannot ask whether there has been a positive yield of the church's investment into the care ministry. A pastor cannot ask if a care ministry has the same (or more) results than another ministry in the church.

The questions of a caring church are, "Has the Lord demonstrated care to us?" "Is the Lord continuing to care for us?" and "Does the Lord's commission to care still apply to us?" The care God is giving us must be utilized to care for others as long as there are people in our community and the world who are in need of our love and care. Have we cared for others as long as God has cared for us? Has His care for us ever stopped?

The Persistence of Care

The church on the corner faithfully conducts its regular meetings for care workers. The first item on the agenda is to remind themselves of the care of God. God was caring for the needy before they were touched by the care of the church. He was caring for the poor long after the church intervened. The church drew its strength from the care of God who was their source and their standard for care.

The church and its pastor first began their care ministry by caring for Jim and Johnny. The pastor noticed that more was happening than just two people becoming upset at the church. He took the time to visit with each of them. At first, they did not respond. They continued to mention problem after problem with the church, but the pastor continued to care for and love both of them.

Just as convincing to Jim and Johnny was the care and sensitivity shown by others in the church. Even when Jim and Johnny resisted the expressions of love and care from different believers, they hoped inwardly these expressions would not stop. They did not. Despite what they saw in Jim and Johnny, the body of believers in the church on the corner continued to show the care of Christ to them.

A new spirit of care began in the church on the corner. While the work with the two, and others, continued, the pastor and those within the church were changing. They were becoming more aware of the profound care of God for them. They were learning how blessed it was to care for others, although it was tiring to work extra on Saturdays, getting food to the hungry and clothing to the needy. They were weary of going to the same ones in the community who seemed never to get better. But they found (among others) a couple, Ben and Sharee, who Jim and Johnny had helped before. They ministered persistently, even though there seemed to be little progress.

The church on the corner learned that caring with the same care God had given them is the only way to care enough. His care never runs out or stops; so they discovered that they are able to still care, never running out or stopping, because their care is based on the care of God.

STRATEGIC TRANSFORMATION STEP
Make the 70 x 7 rule the measuring rule
for success in your ministry care.

PROCEDURE TO DEVELOP
Be diligent in giving care,
both inside and outside the church

STRATEGIC TRANSFORMATION STEP
We begin measuring care by God's perspective
of the needy, rather than by the response.

---11---

CARE FOR THE ONE YOU'RE WITH

A church must be aware enough to be present. The church is present at many functions, but tragically it is absent when it comes to delegating care to others. When care is given, people are often not even aware that it comes from the church. Because of the "absence" of the church, they may come to know no more about the church than they previously knew. Care that counts is not even possible without presence; the messenger is important as well as the message. God chose to deliver His care by being present and in relationship with humanity. Without relationship, care is reduced to mere deeds and acts that run counter to the purposes of care.

Do They Know Who Is Doing This?

Alex was afraid when he went with believers

into the neighborhood. It was the middle of a clear day, and several homeless individuals were standing on the street corner. The church had notified the police in the area that they would be engaged in benevolence ministry. In fact, the police knew that every Saturday the church on the corner would be in the neighborhood distributing food and clothing. The Christians visited with individuals as they ministered, distributing items to meet their needs.

Nevertheless, Alex was apprehensive about being in this neighborhood and in this part of town. Questions kept coming to him, *Why am I down here? I don't know these people. What good does this do? These people would be here whether I came out on Saturday or not.* What troubled Alex most was other thoughts — thoughts that made him angry: *These people don't care if I'm here. Anybody could do this. Why can't we just hire somebody to come down here? In fact, I'd be willing to pay somebody else to be here in my place. All that matters is that these people get the food and other stuff we're giving out week after week.*

Suddenly, a voice interrupted Alex's thoughts. "Hi," said the homeless man standing in front of him. Without noticing, Alex had walked right up in front of a man standing on the corner. He was dressed in the kind of clothing street people wear — dirty, torn and in need of repair. Alex stared into the face of a man who needed a shave and a haircut, In fact, just combing his hair would have helped. Alex was surprised by the intrusion into his thoughts. Even more, he was bothered by the man speaking to him.

Alex thought, *Why is he saying something to me? I didn't come down here to talk to anybody. I came to help these people. Don't they appreciate the fact that I sacrificed my Saturday morning? Why doesn't he leave me alone and let me do this "ministry?" Why do I have to say anything to him? I think I'll give him this jacket. It's a cold day, and he doesn't have a coat. If he appreciates it, maybe he'll leave me alone.*

These thoughts flooded his mind as he struggled to respond to this man who wanted to talk to him. Actually, the man just wanted to get to know Alex. Maybe Alex would find out his name was Robert, maybe he wouldn't.

Robert thought, when he first saw Alex, *Who is this dude coming down my street? He looks like a typical church guy, all cleaned up, his head in the air, thinking he's doing us a favor by being here for 15 minutes.* Robert's dad was a preacher, and he had been raised in a church not too far away. But those memories were buried under years of disappointment, rejection and sin.

This guy coming towards Robert looked as though he wasn't paying attention to where he was going. Something about him reminded Robert of his dad. He wasn't sure what it was, but he thought he would say, "Hi," to keep the churchman from running into him. Just before the guy was right in front of him, Robert recognized what it was about this guy that reminded him of his dad — the expression on the man's face. His dad had that same faraway look, especially around Robert. It was as though he

had something else on his mind. He was there with
Robert, but he was somewhere else in thought.

Later in life, Robert found out that his dad always
had the church on his mind. He worried about what
people were saying, all the things he had to do and
a host of other things to do with "ministry." Robert
resented those thoughts, because they took his dad
away from him. His father did all the things dads
are supposed to do, but it was like he was just going
through the motions; there was no real person
inside. After years of wondering, Robert figured
out that what he really wanted was his dad to be
with him, not somewhere else in thought.

The Absentee Church Is Busy

At the church on the corner there are several
Roberts, and they are not all in the youth group. Their
ages vary, but they have something in common—
they are hurting because of neglect. The irony is that
some of the people who get the most attention in the
church are some of the most hurting among us. They
are not hurting for a lack of ministry; the church is
more involved in ministry than ever before. They are
hurting because of a lack of presence—the presence
of mothers, fathers, brothers and sisters in the faith.
They are surrounded by people who minister to them
but who are never with them. Caregivers are physically present, extending a hand of care, but some are
psychologically and spiritually absent, preoccupied
mentally and spiritually with other things.

A lot of folks are like Robert's dad. They are some

of the most involved people in the church. Their involvement is good, but what is missing is their presence. They are so preoccupied with the busyness of care, they fail to care with the most important part of all — their presence. They make sure that acts of care are accomplished within and without the church, but they rarely, if ever, give the most important sacrifice — their presence — to someone in need. Alex is one of these people.

How do you weigh the value of a conversation with someone in which you really communicate a part of yourself, a bit of your personal history, a personal feeling about an issue, a spontaneous reaction? How do you value the importance of just spending time with a person with no real purpose except the relationship? These things communicate our presence: who we are and not just what we do for others. How do you compare letting a person know who you are as a person with meeting their needs?

The greatest need of a person, saint or sinner, is the need for relationship. We all need a saving relationship with God. A believer must come to know God and communicate who she or he is to God. The second greatest need — a need created by God himself — is the need for relationships with others. This is the need to share who we are with another person, and to be open in knowing someone else. The first great need is mirrored in the first great commandment: "You shall love the Lord your God with all your heart, with all your soul, and with all your mind" (Matthew 22:37). The second great need is matched by the second great commandment: "You shall love your neighbour as yourself" (Galatians 5:14).

The church houses many of the the hurting and the absent. The presence of the absent would comfort the hurting. To have ministries of care and be absent to those to whom care is extended is a grievous mistake. A church cannot remain a caring body and keep its presence separated from its acts of ministry, without consequences.

Presence Is Caring

Presence is a caring skill just as real as physical action. In fact, our presence or lack of presence speaks louder than our actions. Who God is completes the acts of God; who we are gives meaning to our acts of care. The act of ministry should leave a definite impression of the man or woman of God who is the caregiver. The presence or absence of the caregiver will linger longer than the care itself.

God communicates His presence as well as His actions. The importance of His presence was communicated when Christ was preparing to leave the earth. In John 13, He broke the news to the disciples that He would no longer be with them physically (vv. 31-35). The disciples had several questions to ask about where He was going and what would they do (see 13:36 – 14:22). Jesus responded by telling them He would be gone physically, but He would still be present. The presence of Jesus would continue in their lives through the presence of the Spirit. For more than two chapters, Jesus shared the revelation

of the Holy Spirit and His own continuing presence
with them through the Spirit (14:23 – 16:33).

A pivotal scripture notes the priority of presence
and relationship in John 15:15: "No longer do I call
you servants, for a servant does not know what his
master is doing; but I have called you friends, for all
things that I heard from My Father I have made known
to you." Jesus was moving the disciples beyond being
servants. As valued as servanthood was to the Master,
it was even more important to know His presence.

Jesus endeavored to communicate the presence
of the Father, but He wanted them to know His
presence as well. He shared with them the relationship He had with the Father so that they could truly
know Him. Christ performed acts of ministry for
the disciples, supplying their needs, but He also
gave them a real sense of Himself and His presence.

The God of All Comfort

Second Corinthians 1:3-5 addresses the need for
communicating our presence to the people to whom
we minister. The word *comfort* is repeated five times
in this passage. It is translated from four different
words in the Greek text. *Paragoreia* is translated
"comfort" in Colossians 4:11. The word means to
"comfort physically, to soothe and bring relief from
pain." *Paramutheomai* is another word translated
comfort and indicates "mental comfort or encourage-
ment in the midst of great need." It was used in
John, 1 Corinthians, 1 Thessalonians and Philemon.
Tharseo is translated "be of good cheer." It indicated

emotional comfort and care. The term is used in all four Gospels and Acts.

The term used in 2 Corinthians 1:3-5 is *parakaleo*. It was constructed from two words which, in combination, mean "to call someone to your side." The physical, mental and emotional levels of care are important, but perhaps the deepest level of comfort and care is conveyed in this term. It indicates comfort by virtue of the presence of another person. This same term is the basis of the name of the Holy Spirit given by Jesus in John 14:26. There Jesus named the Holy Spirit "Comforter." (KJV) In the ancient text, the term was *Paraklete*. Comfort through presence was the deepest level of care, and the primary message Jesus left the disciples on the eve of the Crucifixion.

A caring church, one that utilizes the ministry of the Holy Spirit, is a church aware of the real presence of Jesus. It is able to communicate its own presence to those it cares for as well. A caring church sees its ministry of care and benevolence as more than a service to people; it is friends of Jesus reaching out in love to those in need (see John 15:15). The gift is incomplete, however, unless we are in the gift, too.

Ministering the Presence of Care

In addition to developing a guiding vision (ch. 2), listing its most critical values (ch. 3), equipping its people to minister together (ch. 4), determining who it will reach (ch. 5), training in the ministries of compassion (ch. 6), holding itself accountable for care (ch. 7), developing policies and procedures that match its intentions to minister to the poor, the needy and the hurting (ch. 8), including those who are not like us (ch. 9), and measuring the success of care by the 70 x 7 rule of Matthew 18 (ch. 10), the church must also minister its presence through the ministry of care.

The care of the church is for individuals, by individuals. A caring church is more than an institution giving to other faceless institutions. Rather, it is people giving to people. The presence of the church must accompany its care. If the recipients do not receive a sense of the presence of the church, the work of the church has not reached the true level of genuine care.

As a member of the church, ask yourself, "Is our care accompanied by our presence? Do the people we care for know enough about us as a church? What do they know about us as individuals? Is our care an expression of our institution, or is it an expression of ourselves?"

Alex Cares for Robert, but Will He Meet Him?

Alex was at a crossroads. Robert had taken the first step, and Alex had to choose whether to give him the coat or whether to give him a part of himself. He could give the coat, return the greeting and walk away. He could go further; he could tell them his name. He could ask Robert *his* name. He could spend some time with Robert on that cold but sunny Saturday. He might even find out about Robert's dad. That would be important because Robert's greatest need was the healing of a hurt he still harbored concerning his absentee dad.

The coat would warm Robert's body, but time spent with him just might save his soul.

STRATEGIC TRANSFORMATION STEP
Make the ministry of the "presence"
of the church primary in caring.

PROCEDURE TO DEVELOP
Get to know the needy, while conveying
who we are to them.

IMPLICATIONS FOR CARE
The church's "presence" is able to minister care,
regardless of the need.

────── 12 ──────
OUT OF MIND, OUT OF MINISTRY

Often the church forgets to care. Care becomes an afterthought, or an occasional case of bad conscience. The last footnote of the budget is the column committed to care. This ministry is done among people, but the business of the church may not be as much about people as it may be about preserving an institution. The priorities of a group of people are reflected in what occupies the minds of the people. Many churches think about personal goals, but not corporate care. Care must be a preoccupation of the mind if it is to become a burden of the heart. Care must be "minded" in order to avoid being neglected.

Turn Out the Lights but Not the Caring
The time has come at the church on the corner, as it does after each service, to turn out the lights. The people have been greeted, both coming and

going. There have been interludes in the service in which people greet one another, exchange handshakes, and give and receive an occasional hug. Songs have been sung, prayers prayed, a sermon preached, time spent at the altar. As the lights go out, the work of the church ends for another week. Or does it?

Immediately, no doubt, you would respond by saying that the work of the church is ongoing, even after the lights go out. True, but do the people filing out of the church really think about caring and ministry the rest of the week? What do they think of during the other six and a half days of the week? What preoccupies their minds most of the time? Do the people leaving the church really remember the time spent in church services as being what binds them to each other and prepares them to be a caring church?

In reality, much of the time spent thinking about church and caring for others is limited to the time spent within the church building. When believers leave the church, the lights of their memories also go out. They minds are preoccupied with many things, such as work, home, recreation and a host of other subjects. These other thoughts are not necessarily bad in and of themselves. But when do they think about the people in need of care, in need of a life change, in need of restoration to Christ and the church?

The most powerful thoughts are frequently those that occupy our minds while we aren't necessarily thinking about anything in particular. These are thoughts we do not have to think; they just drift across our minds when we are doing something else. They stay in our minds much of the time. These floating thoughts are generally what we care about the most. The things and people forgotten by us during the week are things and people we neglect, intentionally or unintentionally.

Unfortunately, church in general and care in particular falls between the cracks and crevices of our minds into the abyss of neglect. If asked, we would respond by saying that we care about the needy and one another. And, in reality, we do care, genuinely, about the needy and one another. The problem is that we forget about care more that we remember it. This forgetfulness does not mean the church doesn't care; it means the church only cares one day a week. The preoccupation of the mind reflects the priority of the person.

Remembering the Goal of Restoration

Because the church neglects to care for others, one of the greatest casualties is restoration. Restoration is the forgiving of a person and the effort to bring him or her back into redemptive fellowship with God and the church. It is a very important aspect of a caring church. Restoration can be pictured as not just rescuing a drowning person, but actually pulling him or her back into the boat. This forgetting not only robs the church of its ability to care, but it robs it of its capacity to restore.

Restoration to the Lord is the first goal of care. Restoration to the body of Christ is the second critical goal of care. Those who have themselves experienced the restoration of the Lord and others are best empowered to care.

The person in need of restoration thinks constantly about what it would be like to be brought back into a right relationship with God and fellowship with the church; but the church itself, unfortunately, barely notices the struggling individual who is in need of restoration.

Those in need of restoration have committed some sin or act that has broken fellowship with God and the community of faith. The person on the road to restoration takes the first steps in the "coming back," restorative process. He or she repents of the sin and seeks to live a purified life. The individual has a desire to come back into the fellowship of God and the church. The thoughts of restoration and the joys of being renewed in fellowship preoccupy the hungry heart.

Sadly, many churches limit their thoughts of the restored to when the lights of the church are on. During the service, when the church gathers together, people who need to be restored cross their minds. But when the lights are out and church is over, they fail to think of the care it takes to restore them.

Giving to Restore

A caring church does not forget those in need of restoration. Every act is another restorative move that draws the hurting closer to God. The distribution of food, the counsel of the heart, the clothing of the barren, the sheltering of the homeless and countless other acts of care are not neutral. They are given with the hope of restoration in mind. This would appear to be obvious, but forgetfulness makes care a business, a mere project or a salve to a troubled conscience. Mindfulness of restorative care, on the other hand, fuels creativity, energizes workers and fulfills discipleship.

The restorative mindset of a caring church requires complete involvement, especially the focus of the mind. The mind directs the actions of the body and reflects the condition of the heart. The mind warns one of impending danger and assures the individual of a job well done. The mind can also deceive the sinner into a justification of sin and lull the saint into a forgetful state of insensitivity. Finally, the mind can direct an entire church away from care, especially the pivotal need for restoration.

Restoration completes so much of the work of God. Forgiveness finds its fulfillment in restoration. Affection blossoms into love through restoration. Salvation is secure because of restoration. Knowledge finds clarity in restoration. Spiritual gifts are applied when there is restoration. The fruit of the Spirit is manifested by restoration. And care reaches its culmination when restoration takes place.

The Ripening of the Fruit and Repairing of the Wall

Galatians 5:19—6:2 shows that the fruit of the Spirit is manifested by restoration. The fruit of the Spirit is contrasted to the lust of the flesh (5:15-18). Manifestations of the lust of the flesh are listed in verses 19-21; the various aspects of the fruit of the Spirit are listed in verses 22 and 23. As a list of the outward works of the flesh follow the inward lust of the flesh, so we would expect a list of the outward results of living in the Spirit. The only work of the fruit of the Spirit listed is restoration (6:1).

Paul's appeal is to the spiritual: "Brethren, if a man is overtaken in any trespass, you who are spiritual restore such a one in a spirit of gentleness, considering yourself lest you also be tempted." Restoration is to be surrounded by the bearing of others' burdens as well as our own (vv. 2-8). This emphasis climaxes a topic Paul introduced in 5:14, "For all the law is fulfilled in one word, even in this: 'You shall love your neighbor as yourself.'" The fruit of the Spirit is especially evident as we bear the burdens of others, and ripens when we restore someone after they have fallen.

Restoring a life is like repairing or rebuilding a wall. In Isaiah 58, the prophet was used by the Lord to challenge the people of God to care. God said in verse 6 that His people were to reach out to those in need. In verse 10, the process of caring was described as extending your soul to care for someone in need. He illustrates it with the restoration of a repaired wall. Once a fortress of protection and safety, the wall had been broken and had become a heap of rubble. To those who care enough to restore, the prophet said, "You shall be called the Repairer of the Breach, the Restorer of Streets to Dwell In" (v. 12). They would be the rebuilders of the broken places.

Restoration is the ripening of the fruit of the Spirit and the repairing of the wall of a city. Care reaches its climax in restoration just as fruit reaches its full maturity and productivity when it is ripe. Care is completed in restoration just as a wall is fully protective when all the broken places have been repaired. Restoration brings care to its fullness. The tragedy of forgetfulness is that the first thing we forget is other people, and people are the objects of restoration.

Remembering Until We Restore

In addition to developing a guiding vision (ch. 2), listing its most critical values (ch. 3), equipping its people to minister together (ch. 4), determining who it will reach (ch. 5), training in the ministries of compassion (ch. 6), holding itself accountable for care (ch. 7), developing policies and procedures that match its intentions to minister to the poor, the needy and the hurting (ch. 8), including those who are not like us (ch. 9), measuring the success of care by the 70 x 7 rule of Matthew 18 (ch. 10), and ministering the presence of the church in the ministry of care (ch. 11), the church must also culminate care by restoring the needy to God as well as the body of believers.

No one likes unfinished business. A half-baked loaf of bread, a race only half run and a game not fully finished are examples of only halfway completing a task. Care is not fully realized until restoration has taken place. A church must elevate restoration as the goal at the end of the race. Care must not be focused on the supplying of temporal needs and then forgotten when the lights of the church are turned off at the end of a service. A church must be consumed with the "finish line" of restoration.

As goals of care ministries are formed, restoration must be seen as the ultimate goal and must thread its way through every goal statement. While different people are challenged about various aspects of caring in the church, the restoration of the fallen must unify all of our care efforts. Restoration is the proof you have been truly spiritual and are truly a caring church. When the church gathers workers together for ministering care, the consciousness of restoration must weigh upon them as they bear the burdens of care.

The church must create an environment of restoration through its caring spirit, its goals and its work. A person who has fallen into poverty, tumbled into catastrophe or slipped into sin will feel welcome to come to a caring church. In a caring church believers will not look down at the needy, but they will renew their perspective of life. They do not put down the hurting, but rather they will lift them up. The caring church is where the needy will not be left alone, forgotten and neglected. It is the place where the restored will be affirmed, remembered and respected.

The steps of restoration, including forgiveness, acceptance and healing, should be given prominent emphasis in the local church. The theme of ultimate restoration must be held up by the church's organization to its people so that they will not forget it. It is so easy for even a caring church to forget its central mission, ultimate goal and desired state. That purpose is to fully connect all of its care to the single goal of restoration. This includes financial restoration, vocational restoration, relational restoration and spiritual restoration.

After the Lights Go Out

When the lights go out in the caring church, after the services are over and the people have left the building, the light of restoration still burns. The fruit of the Spirit glows brightly as the caring church continues to be a restorative community. The repair of broken walls continues as the church bridges the gap between those in need and the people of the church.

The members at the church on the corner were not satisfied only to do acts of care. They strive to culminate those acts with seeing lives truly changed. They long to see homes mended once again. They yearn to have the poor restored vocationally. They are hungry to have those alienated by society brought into the healing community of believers. They are not only stirred to have individuals brought to a fresh meal, but also to a restored relationship with the Savior and with their church.

STRATEGIC TRANSFORMATION STEP
View the goal of care as the restoration of
persons to God and the body of believers.

PROCEDURE TO DEVELOP
Aim to restore, rather than punish
or provide a temporary solution.

IMPLICATIONS FOR CARE
True spirituality in a church is evidenced
by the restoration of the needy and fallen.

—————————— 13 ——————————

THE BOTTOM LINE IS A CROSS

——————————

A church must care enough to sacrifice. Most congregations are fearful of any kind of decline, any backward look or reflective retreat. As a result, the efforts toward aggressive growth and self-preservation leave care in a woeful trail of dust. A church can make temporary progress while its care ministry declines.

Waiting on those who need our care requires patience and sacrifice. The ability to sacrifice prompts us to slow down and wait for those who need our care. Those who need care are slower, weaker and less able to keep up. The movement toward the needy and the searching may cause a stepback or delay for the upwardly mobile church. The church will move at a different pace if it takes the time to be sensitive to care.

Would There be Room Today?
What if Mary and Joseph walked up to the

153

church on the corner with an armload of kids—
would there be room in the church for them? Or what
if Mary kept coming although she was pregnant, and
not all the questions about her pregnancy, her fiancé
and her future had been answered? Would you make
room on your pew in your church for her to sit? What
if Mary and Joseph did not show up at the front door
of the church, but you just heard about a couple in the
community looking for food, clothing and shelter . . .
would there be a team from your church to reach
them? Finally, would Mary, Joseph and Jesus even
cross your mind, or would they be put in the animal
stall in the back part of your mind?

A couple came to the church on the corner one
night. Their clothes were old and out of date. Their
car was still older, and looked completely out of
place in the parking lot. They came asking for food
rather than for a place to sit. They told a story that
seemed almost unbelievable about how they ended
up in poverty and displaced from their home. They
didn't have anything to put in the offering or contribute to any of the ministries, and had little to say
except, "Help."

A man also came to church who had been driven
out of a nearby town by gossip. He was hoping no
one at the church would know who he was, or
notice that he looked suspicious. But he was talkative
enough to be noticed by a few people who went out
to eat with others after church. He was recognized by
still others as the man in the newspaper who had
been accused of questionable acts and held by the
police for a short time.

A woman came to church that Sunday who was trying to raise three children on her own. She was holding on to two jobs and trying to keep the family from being separated. She had a tired look; and had neglected her appearance, as well as the looks of her children. The crowd seemed to part to the left and the right as they walked down the hallway and out of the building. Her children had been unruly and kept interrupting the teacher in Sunday school. She bothered one of the ushers long enough to ask him if the church had a food pantry.

Someone in the church on the corner had the idea that he would go this week to the other side of town and pick up some children for Sunday school. The children came in all shapes and sizes. Some only had one parent, others had no parents, and still others did not know who their parents were. They kept looking around at the church, pointing to the building and furniture, making a spectacle of themselves. Some even ran when they should have walked, stood when they should have sat and talked when they should have been quiet.

It was almost as if God was asking, "Is there room in the church for these?"

When the Church Is an Inn and You Are Left Out

Today the church often fails to care because it is unwilling to sacrifice. Care never contributes, it takes from a church. The needy never deposit, they only withdraw from the church. The poor are not givers, but survivors who make demands on the church's time, finances and activities. The church on the corner was a comfortable place for believers to stay a few hours of the week — much like a nice motel. They made sure that all the comforts were present, and the number one priority was the pleasant stay of each believer during worship. If the church on the corner was a cozy inn of religious ritual, then the odds are that it had Marthas, Josephs and children who had been asked to not bother the "guests."

The theme of sacrifice ultimately makes us look to the Cross. The world was changed by One who hung there. The souls of humanity were offered salvation by One who spoke through silence. The suffering of humanity was lifted by One who suffered with them. The injustices of the world were righted by One who did not rail at His accusers. The poor of the world were made rich by One who left the riches of His eternal home. The hungry received the Bread of Life from One who did not compete with the powerful. The thirsty received living water from One who didn't resist when He was made to taste vinegar. The ill and diseased received healing from One who stood still under the pain of repeated stripes.

The world was not changed by someone running a race; it didn't receive everlasting care from someone in a competition to be the best. The world was not moved by someone trying to get ahead. In the same manner, the world will not be loved, cared for and restored by a church continually occupied with becoming larger, earning more and being more influential. The church's influence is designed after

Calvary's hill, not Capitol Hill. The church's stewardship is the result of the price paid on the cross, not a price raised in a bidding war for talent. The church's size is as large as the sacrifice on Golgotha, not the crowds that come to see but not to commit themselves.

The church must learn the way of sacrifice taught by the Christ on the cross. His sacrifice was the ultimate act of compassion. It provides the template by which Christian care is formed. The total sacrifice of Christ made our total provision possible. He steadfastly fixed His eyes on the Cross—a way so different from what the world requires for success. The Cross was Christ's giving up Himself in order to minister life to others. In the same way, the church must learn to sacrifice itself in order to empower its care.

He Came to Die as Our Sacrifice

The world was searching for a caring Savior. Sin had separated humanity from God. Men and women were lost, seeking One who would care for their souls. The Savior came as a mighty warrior, defeating the power of the Enemy. He came as a King with authority to overcome the rule of Satan. He came in mercy and grace, purchasing the sinners' redemption. All of these forms of the Savior's work, however, became available when He gave Himself as a sacrifice on the cross.

In the same manner, all that the church has to offer the world comes together in the church's sacrifices. Christ giving Himself on the cross is the model of sacrifice for the caring church. The various elements of a caring church discussed in this book become realities when the church follows the example of Christ on the cross. The Cross represents both care to the church and care flowing from Christ through the caring church. In this book, I have emphasized some of the elements of the Savior sacrificing Himself on the cross:

- He was focused on the vision of sacrifice and care.

- He reflected the values and priorities of the heavenly Father's heart of care.

- He provided gifts of equipping and ministry through the Cross.

- He reached out to all who would receive Him through the Cross.

- He trained and modeled compassion for His disciples by way of the Cross.

- He gave Himself on the cross as the guarantee of His care to the world.

- He carried out the intentions of the Godhead for care through His sacrifice on the cross.

- He came from His heavenly home to sacrifice Himself for those who were not like Him.

- He exercised the 70 x 7 principle in laying down His life for the reconciliation of the those who desire to be saved.

- After the Cross, He promised never to leave the believer.

- In giving Himself on the cross, He reconciled all who would believe on Him.

- He made sacrifice the model of care when He gave Himself on the cross.

The Tender Shepherd and the Good Samaritan

Isaiah 40:10, 11 describes the Savior in two essential ways. First, He is described as a mighty warrior in verse 10. He has all strength, power, authority and might. He is the mighty victor, prophetically proclaimed. Out in front, He leads His victorious army.

Verse 11 gives the second description: He is a gentle shepherd. Here, He is at the back of the line; He is at the back of the mighty army. He is helping the tender lambs who are too fragile to keep up. He carries them in His bosom. He gently leads those who are with young.

His care takes Him, sacrificially, all the way back to the end of the victory processional to make sure all His children are cared for.

Jesus illustrated this care in the story of the Good Samaritan. A man, like the tender Shepherd of the Cross, took a sacrificial step backward to care for someone who had fallen. The Samaritan was on a journey, and the man by the wayside had already been bypassed by busy travelers. Some were on a religious journey for a spiritual cause. But the Samaritan took time, retraced his steps and stooped down for someone in need. As a personal sacrifice, he took more time, gave up his travel plans and provided his own funds to ensure the restoration of a fallen traveler. Like Jesus, the Samaritan led by going back and sacrificing.

In the same way, the church sometimes follows the path of care by leaving forward-looking plans, sacrificing its time, altering its plans and giving of its finances to restore the needy. The move to the back of the line and personal sacrifice are both required if we are to be a caring church. The suffering Savior who gave Himself as a sacrifice for our care is the church's example that leads it back to the needy.

Step Back In Order To Step Forward

In addition to developing a guiding vision (ch. 2), listing its most critical values (ch. 3), equipping its people to minister together (ch. 4), determining who it will reach (ch. 5), training in the ministries of compassion (ch. 6), holding itself accountable for care (ch. 7), developing policies and procedures that match its intentions to minister to the poor, the needy and the hurting (ch. 8), including those who are not like us (ch. 9), measuring the success of care by the 70 x 7 rule of Matthew 18 (ch. 10), ministering the presence of the church in the ministry of care (ch. 11), and culminating care with the restoration of the needy with God and the body of believers (ch. 12), the church must see the sacrifice of Christ on the cross as the ultimate mentor for the caring church.

The caring church looks backward as well as forward. Making sure not one is left behind keeps us more centered than always marching ahead. The search for a caring church is risky, painful and a somewhat "backward" movement, in the sense that the church may have to stay behind to care for the needy while others seem to make great strides forward. But that may be where the forward movement of the church really is—a caring move to wait for those who cannot keep pace with the rest of society.

The movement of the caring church is toward the neighbor, even if it means not getting to Jerusalem as fast, even if it means self-sacrifice. The various steps involved in becoming a caring church have been described at the end of each chapter. All of these steps can be summarized by the church's need to follow Christ, who is our mentor of care.

Care is more an act of devotion than it is an act of benevolence.

- When the church cares, it serves the Savior.

- When the church cares, it fulfills the call to discipleship.

- When the church cares, it lifts up praises to God.

- When the church cares, it demonstrates the love of Christ.

- When the church is caring, it is most fully the church.

The Savior Is Searching for a Caring Church

Jesus is at the doorstep of the church just as He was in the womb of Mary, waiting with Joseph to see if there was room for them in the inn. The

Savior, in the form of the poor, the destitute and the needy of the world, is looking for a caring church. The church is filled with people who are tired, discouraged and disillusioned. They, in turn, are waiting for the church to emerge as a genuine community, embracing one another in order to care. Care is the doorway to every ministry of the church—to those outside and within its walls.

Our Lord sees the searching. He sees every tear. Songwriters Scott Kippayne and Steve Siler aptly capture the reality of the searching Savior:

> You feel insignificant—
> A whisper in the wind;
> Sometimes you think nobody knows your name.
> But there's somebody watching over you
> And He knows everything you're going through.
>
> He sees every single tear,
> He feels everything you're feeling,
> He wants to hold you close and dry your eyes.
> Your heart is what He hears
> When the world just hears you crying,
> No matter what the pain, He cares
> About every single tear.
>
> Overwhelmed by circumstances
> Out of your control—
> Hope can be the hardest thing to find.
> When you're like a heart without a home
> You don't have to face this hurt alone.
>
> If God adorns the lilies of the field

And cares for every sparrow in the sky,
How much more is He aware of your sorrow and despair?
How much does He care about your life?

"Every Single Tear" by Scott Krippayne and Steve Siler. Copyright © 1997

At every service and in every ministry throughout the week, the church is making decisions about care. We do not need to go out and see if anyone is interested in care; the searchers are already there—waiting, looking, for a caring church.

The decision is not for those in need; they have already made their decision and are searching for a caring church. The decision is yours—whether to be a caring church, not just a church with care ministries.

STRATEGIC TRANSFORMATION STEP
Make Christ on the cross the ultimate
mentor for believers in the caring church.

PROCEDURE TO DEVELOP
Make the message from the Cross the
ultimate message of your church.

STRATEGIC TRANSFORMATION STEP
There is triumph for the redeemed through
the care Jesus showed at the cross.